Having known Cheryl most of my li[...] her in many facets of life. Each facet has chiseled, carved, and sometimes crushed her, resulting in the igniting of her inner core, bringing to the surface her true, brilliant colors.

Cheryl carries a torch—a torch that has melted those crushed minerals of her life into eye-catching gems, filled with the sparkle of hope, strength, and clarity. Dark times enter everyone's life and can be viewed as either invaluable or valueless. The decision is ours and needs to be made, knowing that "not to decide is to decide."

Cheryl's torch-bearing quest will leave you captivated and intrigued as she describes her life's maze, pointing you toward changing who you are, not what you're going through. *Wave by Wave* is a must read for those souls looking to self-excavate and find those gems needing to be illuminated.

—**Sandy Dow Haga**, South Haven, MI

Cheryl Tinsley was a wonderful student of mine and a player on one of my teams when I was a science professor and women's basketball coach at Cornerstone University. After she left the university to begin her career as a teacher and park ranger, she returned often to Lake Ann Camp to share her story and life lessons learned. I was privileged to see the individuals, young and old, challenged to make their lives matter. God's ways are not our ways. He chose to save Cheryl from the fingers of the icy lake. In this book, you'll discover the author's transparency, courage, and faith in a God who sees and saves.

—**Ray Gates**, PhD, professor emeritus, Cornerstone University

I have been a featured speaker at Lake Ann Camp for the Senior High Program for thirty-five summers. During the twentieth summer of my experience at Lake Ann Camp, a former counselor, Cheryl Tinsley, came to visit. After my wife and I heard the story of her experience of being a counselor at Lake Ann and her story of survival on Lake Huron, we knew she had to share it with the senior high students. For the last fifteen years Cheryl has come back to Lake Ann to share her story. The campers listen to her amazing story in complete attention and identify with Cheryl in a special way. God is with Cheryl as she shares her story and we believe He has helped her tell it in this book. May the Lord use it in your life to find Him as a Good God, a Faithful God, a Deliverer, and a Miracle Worker!

—**Ken and Jinner Rudolph**, ABWE missionaries (retired)

WAVE
by
WAVE

WAVE
by
WAVE

A Memoir of Survival,
Faith, and How God Works

Cheryl Steele Tinsley

AS TOLD TO A. L. ROGERS

credo
house publishers

Published in the United States by Credo House Publishers,
a division of Credo Communications LLC, Grand Rapids, Michigan
credohousepublishers.com

ISBN: 978-1-62586-242-6

Cover design and interior layout by Frank Gutbrod
Editing by Emily Irish

Printed in the United States of America

First Edition

CONTENTS

INTRODUCTION

I thought in the sixth grade that I was going to be a teacher. Now, it's been almost thirty years since I took attendance for the first time in my first class ever. The school keeps asking me to come back, so I must be doing something right. I love students and I've always been good at relating to people. My students tell me that I'm "real," and I think they like that. Even the hardcore kids that other people can't deal with will come to me. "Cuz you're *real* Mrs. T." I think they know that if they come to me, I'll tell it to them straight.

I'm also a storyteller. Big groups make me a little bit nervous, like they do for anyone, but after I work the nerves out I can usually tell some good stories. I like to tell stories that encourage people and make them laugh. I also like to tell stories that maybe teaches a little something too, or at least gets them to stop and think.

The story you're about to read is one that I've been telling since the summer of 1980. I'm the main character, and yet I'm not. This is a story about four incredible young adults and the loving communities around them. This is also a story about God.

I don't assume that everyone who picks up this book believes in God. But whether you do or not, I hope you'll give this story a chance. I believe the Creator God is active in the world today, and I've got a story about how I've seen Him in action.

I'm going to tell it to you straight, just like I do with my students!

PART I

CALM BEFORE *the* STORM

FAST LEARNER

In 1978, I was a student at Pensacola Christian College in Pensacola, Florida. I was studying nursing at the time, and at first I loved it. It was during my freshman year, and the next two summers, that I first saw death. I don't think I grew comfortable with death. Can anyone really grow comfortable? However, those encounters would matter a great deal later in my life.

In addition to my studies, I was a nurse's aide when school was out. During the summers after my senior year of high school and after my freshman year of college, I worked in geriatric care at a place called Inter-City Manor in Allen Park, Michigan. It was a good job for those two summers. I thought I wanted to go into nursing—I liked helping people. I didn't know it then, but I now believe God was using that job to prepare me for the ordeal I would face later on in my life.

Inter-City Manor was set up like an apartment building, and I knew it well. It was attached to the grounds of the high school I graduated from, Inter-City Christian School. The manor was like a high-rise retirement village, nestled in a Detroit suburb. Since the organization didn't have land to expand on at that time, they just kept building up. It was ten stories high, and I worked on the second floor. The second floor was where someone could live if they got sick and needed care for the rest of their life. There were also three meals a day served on the second floor. So, all the Inter-City residents would come from other floors for their meals and to socialize before heading back to their apartments. Daily, I was able to engage with all the residents during meals.

I enjoyed seeing older people come and go on the second floor. I got to know many of them. God blessed me with a sense of humor that can find something to chuckle about in almost any situation. I so enjoyed laughing and talking with the residents, and I think they liked our conversations too. Unfortunately, some of the folks I encountered during those summers died. I was just a teenager, but when someone would pass away, I and other staff members were responsible for preparing the body to be taken to the funeral home.

Emergency situations were fairly common at Inter-City. We were caring for elderly people, many of them sick and facing life-threatening issues. Emergency situations are a regular part of geriatric care. In these situations, you have to move *fast*. We were trained and certified in first aid, CPR, and other emergency treatments. When someone who was under our care needed immediate help, the nurse's aides would call for the head nurse while rushing to lend a hand.

Though it became clear to me after my first year at Pensacola that God was *not* calling me to be a nurse, I believe now that He was preparing me for what I would experience in one of the hardest nights of my life.

ELDON "DAD" BROCK

After two summers in geriatric care, I knew I wanted a new work experience for the upcoming summer of 1979. It was the springtime, and I was a sophomore at Grand Rapids Baptist College (GRBC, now called Cornerstone University) back in my home state of Michigan. I'd left the nursing program at Pensacola and was considering what else God might have for me. I knew He didn't want me to be a nurse. Teaching as a career became more and more interesting. Perhaps sixth grade Cheryl knew all along what I was destined to do. Whatever was coming next, I knew I wanted to do something different.

Every year, the college would host a Spring Renewal Conference, which was always a special time. The conference included a series of speakers (many of them well-known Bible teachers of the day) as well as outside activities and competitions between dormitories. (It was a fun time of activities, food, and fellowship!) The school would also allow ministries and other organizations to come in, set up tables in a designated area in the gym, and talk to students who might be interested in working for them.

During that Spring Renewal, I met someone who would become a trusted mentor and a lifelong friend. Mr. Eldon Brock was the director of the Regular Baptist Camp at Lake Ann.

Mr. Brock had already filled all of the counselor positions, but he was looking to hire an "assistant wilderness director," someone who would help the lead wilderness director take campers on excursions around Michigan's beautiful woodlands and lakes. So, I—a girl raised in the suburbs of Detroit with five other kids in one house (three older sisters, JoAnn, Carolyn, and Linda, and two younger brothers, Earl and Jim)—started talking to this camp director about becoming his assistant wilderness director.

Eldon asked me, "Do you have any experience camping?"

Always quick to make a joke, I said, "Well, I have nice-sized backyard and I camp out there sometimes." He smiled and I told him about growing up not far from Detroit in the Melvindale, Allen Park area. We were a blue-collar family. Both my parents worked for General Motors and didn't have a lot of extra money, or even extra time, to take six kids camping. We had a small backyard that didn't make much of a campsite. I can only imagine he looked at me and at first saw a city kid, not an assistant wilderness director.

But good-natured Eldon started chuckling and asked, "Do you have experience being out on the water, in lakes? We do quite a bit of swimming. And what about rafting or canoeing?"

"Well," I joked again, "does gluing together popsicle sticks and floating them in a big bathtub count? Because I'm really good at that!" He started laughing again. My chances of landing this job suddenly felt about as good as the chances that one of my popsicle rafts would survive a trip down the Detroit River.

"Look, Mr. Brock," I said. "I love the outdoors. I love to hike. I actually hope to do summer seasonal work at national parks when I get older." Then I promised him, "If you give me a chance, I'm a fast learner."

"Cheryl, I love your personality. I love your spunk," he said. He then handed me an application. "Why don't you fill this out? I have a feeling I'll be calling you in the next week or two."

Fortunately, Eldon felt my love for the Lord, sense of humor, and positive attitude made me just what he was looking for in a staff member at Lake Ann. God had opened the door for me to work with young people in His beautiful outdoor arena. I had never been to camp before 1979. The first time I ever set foot in a camp of any kind was at Lake Ann. But I absolutely fell in love with the work that summer. It solidified a lifetime love for the outdoors and for working with students.

Dear Mr. Brock,   recd 4-30-79   4/24/79

Hello, my name is Cheryl Steele. I heard about Regular Baptist Camp through some friends of mine Nancy Tanis, and Dee Fail. I would be very interested in working this summer as a counselor at your camp.

At the present, I am attending Pensacola Christian College and majoring in Nursing. I'm a transfered sophomore, and last year I attended Bob Jones University in Greenville, S.C. I am from Michigan and live in Melvindale (a suburb outside of Detroit). I was wondering if you could please send me an application if some positions are still available.

P.S. You are becoming well-known in Pensacola, Fla!

Thank you for your time!

Sincerely,

Cheryl Steele

A letter I sent to Eldon Brock after our initial meeting at the Spring Renewal Conference.

WILDERNESS
COUNSELORS

One of the reasons Eldon Brock hired me is because he needed a balance of male and female wilderness directors, and at the time, he needed another female on the team. The reasons for this are obvious: an even mix of both men and women to lead the campers were needed for what were often co-ed groups of teens.

The two male wilderness counselors during the summer of 1979 were Dwight Herzberger and Jeff Tindall. Both were Lake Ann veterans. Dwight had worked there for the previous six years, while Jeff had started in 1974. Over the course of that summer, all of our personalities clicked. We became like siblings and worked well together.

We underwent three weeks of intense training in survival skills and first aid safety before heading out to raft, bike, or backpack with campers who wanted a bigger challenge. Our job as wilderness counselors was to take campers on weeklong bike trips across Northern Michigan or whitewater rafting on the Pine River.

This is the wilderness crew of 1979, along with three campers. We stopped for lunch near Fisherman's Point on The Mighty Pine River. I am on the right. Dwight Herzberger is wearing the hat. Jeff Tindall is in the bottom left.

During the school year Dwight taught English at Jackson Christian High School. He carried his love for words beyond the classroom, too. I regularly saw Dwight writing in a journal that summer. I also learned that he was letter writer to friends and family too. These were handwritten letters, produced with time and attention long before emails and text messages ever existed. Dwight was gifted with words!

Here's an excerpt from one of Dwight's letters to a friend. I love how his personality and his authentic commitment to following God's plan for his life surfaces in these words. This excerpt also describes some of the life and work of a wilderness counselor.

I haven't been into the Word as much as I wanted to be this week. I had almost all day yesterday to myself and spent most of that time messing around. Dave and I played some games such as "bomb the ship." You throw a big piece of wood in the lake and throw stones at it until it's either broken to bits or out of range. We skipped stones for who knows how long. I found it amazingly easy to keep myself idle.

Friday Afternoon

Success always tastes so sweet. We have spent the entire afternoon rock-climbing, and I have never seen a group of guys eat it up as much as they do. It never fails to amaze me how excited I am after climbing a cliff. One of my guys, Brent Sneider, is a natural goat. You wouldn't believe it unless you saw it. Dan Nifer, C.J.'s brother, got up 5 feet off the ground and froze. It's amazing what a few feet off the ground will do to your coordination. When you see my slides, you'll understand a lot more completely what I've written. What I have written is only a fragment of the thoughts, feelings, and activities that have occurred during the past week. That's obvious. But I hope through this somewhat incomplete account you'll understand to a greater degree what I do out here and what I'm like.

I wonder what I look like. I haven't seen my face in a week. I haven't washed my hair since last Saturday night. I hope I don't look as bad as I smell. My beard is feeling thicker, but I'm afraid it still looks scraggy. It's funny to see the zits on everyone else, and not realize you have them too. I'm going to read in 1 Corinthians and take a nap before we return to the ridge for more climbing.

Saturday—Solo

It's late afternoon and very, very cold and windy. It started raining this morning about two hours before dawn. That lasted off and on till 7:00. It's really a beautiful day to be on the island. Gigantic waves have been thundering in all day. The wind has forced me to remain in my tarp and bag in order to keep warm. I can feel the rocks below me rumble when the monster waves hit shore. It's impossible to start a fire. The wind gusts up to 15–20 mph and never eases below 10 mph. I'm super comfortable in my little lean-to. I have a tree trunk extending toward the lake across a depression in the shoreline. I have a smaller tree trunk running across it to form a capital T. My tarp is laid across the T-frame giving me about 2 1/2 feet of head clearance at one end and zero at the other. The wind blows over the tarp making it possible for me to keep warm and dry inside.

I've been in here since 8:00 this morning. For the past 6 hours I've listened to the wind, waves, seagulls, and my rain poncho insanely flap in the wind. Though I've dozed off a few times, I've been able to relax and think a lot.

I've thought a lot about what kind of person I am to the young people I minister to during the Summer. I contemplate on how God uses my free and open style to relax me and others in tense situations. I simply won't allow myself to get uptight over a whole lot of things. Sometimes

I think I'm too lighthearted for my own good, yet that's the way God made me. I can accept it, but a lot of people can't.

I have wondered what's in store for me in the future. Now that I'm out of college, I no longer have 3 or 4 years of school to fill up my life. I'm contracted to teach one year at a time. I love the independence—not to do my own thing as much, as I'm able to serve God freely with no others to consider. I have a mobility that is rare. I teach 9 months and have my Summers free to do as He pleases. It's a blast!

Yet even with that freedom and all the fun, enjoyment and freedom it gives me to really experience life, I still desire that female companionship that could possibly or most probably would bring to an end the lifestyle I'm living now. I'm not anxious to settle down. In fact, I'm expecting God to bring someone my way who desires a lot of the same things out of life as I do. I'm not a mover as I have been accused. I know better. I'm not that shallow or insecure. I have never been girl crazy. I'm too bashful and awkward to ever make a good impression on a girl when I've tried to impress her.

My feet are getting numb from the cold. I'd put on my other pair of wool socks, but I used them for mittens this morning and they're soaked and filthy with ash. I'll write more later. Right now, I'm going to get my feet back to 98.6°.

It's past 6:00 and it's getting colder. It's down in the low 50°'s if not the high 40°'s. I don't even dare get out of my bag. I've spent the whole day inside (what a joke). The rain comes and goes still. What a pain to crawl out of here when nature calls. It's going to be a long sleepless night. I feel like I have been loafing all day.

Another interesting trait about Dwight Herzberger were his "snorts" and awesome sense of humor. It was like no other. He could get you laughing about anything. We all had lots of "belly laughter" that summer from our lighthearted companion. But there was another side to Dwight, if you really knew him as a person, which revealed a very deep and passionate pursuit of God.

I love the image of Dwight spending all day in a little tarp-covered lean-to, journaling, writing letters, and thinking about how he can serve God best. There is something to be said about getting away from it all, and getting out into nature, where I believe our Creator can touch our hearts.

Dwight Herzberger drying a pair of wet shorts over an open fire. He was always making us laugh!

A SUMMER JOB

One year later and I was looking for another summer job. I'd spent the 1979–1980 academic year at GRBC. I majored in teacher education with concentrations in history and physical education; plus, I played on the school's basketball team, and just enjoyed college life as a twenty-year-old. I loved the outdoors and there was no question that I wanted to work at Lake Ann Camp again!

I was so pleased when "Dad Brock" hired me back as a wilderness counselor. It meant another three months of enjoying God's incredible creation and hopefully stirring the hearts of campers. I couldn't wait.

During these summers, so many kids made decisions to follow Jesus. For a Christian, this means that they confess their sins to God, and they believe that Jesus's death paid the cost of their sins. This confession of sin and faith in Jesus is the beginning of a lifetime relationship with God. It's a profound, often emotional experience that Christians believe secures someone's soul for an eternity with God. We often call this "getting saved" or "making a decision for Christ." Many kids who came to camp were already saved, but for one reason or another, were not living in a way that honors God. These students often rededicated their lives to Jesus Christ during camp. There's just something about being outdoors in God's beautiful creation that makes one reevaluate their choices and turn back to the Creator.

That's what working at camp was all about. I loved to get kids out in God's creation, outside of their normal habitat, and see what would happen. The camp experience usually shows them that they are capable of more than they once thought. They learn about themselves. They experience an authentic camaraderie with others while they are hiking, biking, or canoeing together

REGULAR BAPTIST CAMP

of Michigan, Inc.

LAKE ANN, MICHIGAN

EMPLOYMENT AGREEMENT

This is to confirm the understanding between the Regular Baptist Camp

and **Cheryl Steele** that he/she shall fill the position

of **Wilderness Director** at this camp. They shall serve in this

capacity from **June 14, 1980** through **August 23, 1980** .

He/she will attend the pre-camp training sessions beginning **June 7**

RESPONSIBILITIES OF THE ADMINISTRATION TO THE STAFF MEMBER.

To undertake the expenses of room, board, and insurance.
To provide one free hour per day and from Saturday noon through Sunday
To help the staff member adjust to his responsibilities and to acquai
him with the camp's goals and philosophy.
To supervise and help the counselor in any way that seems advisable.
To pay a salary of $ **450.00** based on **10** weeks.

RESPONSIBILITY OF THE STAFF TO THE CAMP.

To be cooperative member of the staff, contributing in every way poss
to the health, harmony and happiness of the camp family.
To be loyal to the aims, policies, and regulations fo the camp.
To live with the campers as companion and guide and assume some respor
sibility for their spiritual and physical welfare.
To pray for each camper in his care.
To seek to lead unconverted campers to the Saviour.
To help each Christian camper to grow in the Lord by helping him to
learn ways of Bible study and to apply Bible truth.
To be willing to go beyond the call of duty when needed.
To be present at all staff meetings.
To voice any criticism to appointed supervisor first.
To realize that a staff member is to be an example of Christian attitu
speech and behavior at all times but especially with campers.

It is understood that the Administration reserves the right to dismiss
any member of the staff, if the best interests of the Camp demand it.

This agreement is signed prayerfully, understanding that its fulfillme
is to glorify the Lord.

Staff Member *Cheryl S. Steele*   Date

Camp Administrator *R Eldon Brock*   Date 6/3/80

Sign and return one copy to: REGULAR BAPTIST CAMP
of Michigan, Inc.
Lake Ann, MI. 49650

My job for Lake Ann during the summer of 1980, including my
handwritten testimony.

throughout the week. And they are open to considering spiritual matters, like sin, grace, and God's love.

Like I said, I couldn't wait to get back for the summer of 1980. On the Lake Ann job application, the question is posed: "Why would you like to serve at camp?" My answer from 1980 reflects both my spiritual passion for the campers as well as my practical concerns about becoming a teacher someday:

> I love to work with kids, and camp is an excellent time to get to know the young people. Just being able to help them in areas such as spiritual matters and working with them to develop their talents. In turn I would learn from the kids, and it will help me to grow more spiritually, knowing that I am an example to them.

MARK TAUBE

Dwight and I were back on for our weeklong wilderness trips, but unfortunately the third "sibling" in our little group, Jeff Tindall, did not plan to return to Lake Ann that summer.

Jeff's father owned a construction company, and Jeff opted to stay home that summer and work in the family business. It was disappointing that our trio wouldn't be reunited, but Dwight already had someone in mind to take Jeff's place.

Mark Taube was a 17-year-old who recently graduated from Jackson Christian High School, where Dwight taught English. Dwight, who was 27 in 1980, was a friend and a mentor to Mark. Dwight saw in him not only a passion for God, but a knack for the outdoors. He would be a perfect fit at Lake Ann.

Mark was a quiet guy with dark hair and a handsome face. He had an athletic build too. He played soccer, baseball, and ran track for the high school teams. All the girls that came to camp that summer thought Mark was a hunk, and so cute!

During Mark's senior year at Jackson Christian, he won the Athlete of the Year award. According to Mark's father, Dan Taube, Mark got his athletic talent from his mother, who had been a good basketball player, landing a spot on her high school team during her freshman year.

"It was fun to go to his games," Dan told me. "All of us [parents] live a little bit through our children."

Dwight had taken Mark under his wing not only because he was one of Dwight's students, but also because they lived next to each other and knew each other well.

Dan and Donna Taube lived in Jackson, Michigan, because they were employees of New Tribes Mission, a Christian organization dedicated to the training and sending of missionaries around the world. Dan Taube was a contractor who felt called to serve and support the mission of God, to spread the Gospel, by working at New Tribes. The Taube family lived in Jackson during Mark's high school years, between 1976 and 1981. They lived in what was at the time the Bible school building. It was a great place for an athletic kid like Mark to come of age. The building included a gymnasium, a full running track, and lots of space to run around and explore.

Dwight Herzberger happened to rent a room from New Tribes just across the hallway from the Taube family.

"Dwight was kind of like a big kid," Dan Taube said with a chuckle. Dwight and Mark got along well, both in the classroom as teacher and student and outside the classroom as friends.

Dan Taube described Mark's decision to work at Lake Ann in 1980: "He didn't have any plans in particular [for that summer],

Mark Taube's senior picture.

so Dwight said, 'I can probably get you on as my assistant at Lake Ann.'" Dan smiled as he shared this story. "It seemed like a good idea for Mark."

Eldon Brock soon hired Mark.[1] Camp life was a great fit for Mark. The outdoor activities, focus on growing close to God, and time spent with his good friend and mentor set Mark up for an incredible summer.

And for the first few weeks, things went really smoothly. Until they didn't.

DRUMMOND ISLAND

D uring the first week of July, Dwight, Mark, and I were gearing up for another wilderness excursion. We were planning to take another group of teens out on one of our wilderness experiences. The group that was coming wanted an experience canoeing and rock climbing. However, due to the sudden death of the youth director's brother in a motorcycle accident, the church had to cancel the youth trip planned for that week. As we were now free for the week, Dwight decided to take the free days and explore more of Drummond Island to see if we could expand our backpacking and canoeing trips there.

Drummond Island is just off the eastern-most point of Michigan's Upper Peninsula. It is a *beautiful* piece of God's creation. Our initial information told us the island was filled with lush forests, wild terrain that was ripe for hiking, and cliffs and rock faces that (we hoped) wouldn't be too challenging for campers to rappel. Drummond is bordered by rocky beaches but contains numerous inlet lakes and rivers, which grant easy access to most of the interior. Since we had no campers for the week, it would be our job to identify new spots on Drummond for future wilderness excursions.

Dwight, Mark, and I were getting ready to go, but we learned that the fourth wilderness counselor, Sandy Dow, a certified lifeguard, needed to stay back at camp that week for lifeguard duty. We needed an even number of men and women for the trip, but it didn't take long to find a replacement. A new counselor named Sally Coon was asked to join us, and she eagerly said yes. I liked Sally, as we both met at and attended Grand Rapids Baptist College the past school year. She was fun, had a great sense of humor, and enjoyed the outdoors as much as I did.

SALLY COON

Sally was the oldest daughter in her family and the second oldest of eight children overall. As such, it wasn't long until she became like her mom's right hand. The Coon family included five boys and three girls. So, there was always a need for Sally to help.

When Sally was twelve years old, the Coons started a church in Cheboygan, Michigan. At that young age, Sally became the church pianist. Every week she'd learn a new hymn, and that was what they would sing. They just kept adding to what she knew how to play.

She would also play accompaniment for her parents' "special music" in the church services. Sally accompanied the Coons on songs like, "Heaven Came Down and Glory Filled My Soul," "I've Discovered the Way of Gladness," and "Beyond the Sunset." Eventually, the small congregation built their own church building. She was the pianist for many years. What made this especially remarkable is that she had few lessons.

Sally the camp counselor. Having fun during an activity with campers.

Sally was also an entrepreneur, even as a teen. In her high school years, she had a job at a Ford Hardware store. She loved this job. During those years she started making macramé bracelets and necklaces using beads, shark's teeth, and other small trimmings. Her employers must have thought her jewelry was good because they allowed her to have a display case.

I was glad Sally was coming on the trip! With our team of four now assembled, we were ready to go.

THE TRIP TO DRUMMOND

We drove an old van owned by the camp to get to Drummond. It had been fixed up by our "beloved Head of Maintenance," Mike Bush. (Mike and Eva Bush were the best and I enjoyed spending time with them and their family!) Mike outfitted the van in order to transport anything the camp might need. It was wide open inside. There were just two nice bucket seats in the front and then a backseat bench that wasn't very stylish, but it worked. The rest of the back was open for carting around supplies or materials or whatever might be needed.

On the morning of Monday, July 30, we reviewed the weather forecasts for the days of our trip. The whole week was supposed to be beautiful. We strapped two aluminum canoes on top of the van and set out on the four-hour drive across the northern part of the state, crossing the historic Mackinac Bridge into the Upper Peninsula of Michigan, and then headed east to Drummond Island. The summer of 1980 was decades before the time when everyone had their own smartphone. We used paper maps and road atlases for this drive.

There was a specialized hiking store (REI) in Traverse City where we purchased a few supplies before leaving the area. Among the items we purchased were waterproof bags. This was somewhat advanced for the time. I was into photography back then. I had taken a couple of classes in college and really enjoyed what I was learning. So, in addition to my other gear, I'd packed a Cannon 35-millimeter camera. I sealed my camera and film with a number of ziplock bags and, finally, one of the new waterproof bags. I planned to return to Lake Ann with images of the sites we'd scouted.

I snapped this photo of Dwight (l) and Mark (r) on Monday, June 30, 1980, with my Canon, not long before we headed out.

We were traveling with two tents. Each tent held two people: one for the men and one for the women. We also packed Swiss Army knives. Walkie-talkies. Extra clothes. Extra jackets.

Extra shoes. We carried our food, some water as well as water purification kits. We also packed some additional collapsible plastic bags for transporting water as needed. I had the camera in my bag, and, of course, all of us carried Bibles.

Dwight brought along one of his journals on this trip, too. He was always writing. I think it was one way that he felt a connection with God.

All in all, our backpacks were full. We were each probably carrying 30–40 pounds. They were the type of hiker's packs that rested the weight on our hips (as opposed to a typical student's backpack which rests the weight on the shoulders and back). There were also shoulder harnesses and a clip across the chest that secured the pack from falling backwards. We also cinched our sleeping bags to each backpack.

We were trained and well equipped. This was real wilderness hiking and canoeing and I loved every minute of it.

Drummond is the name of both the island and the township on the island. The island is small and absolutely beautiful. Just over a thousand people live on Drummond Island. Much of the land is state owned. It is a perfect location for a wilderness trip with campers. The beauty of God's creation is all around us on Drummond Island. The island has almost 150 miles of shoreline and forty inland lakes. It looked magical and enchanting to me. Such beauty.

We took the short ferry ride over to Drummond. We thought that was cool and captivating to see the gorgeous shoreline. It was rugged, and pristine. Drummond has only one store and not many roads that a car could travel on. We stopped at the general store for food and gas, and then proceeded to the trailhead and parked the van.

We brought freeze-dried food on these wilderness trips. Back at camp, we had a kitchen room set up where we would make oatmeal or other meals and then freeze-dry them in packets for two or four people for our summer trips. This sustenance did its job, but at the store we made sure and bought additional water and snacks. Candy bars and chips are divine on the trail and are morale boosters!

PART II

FREAK STORM

JULY 3, 1980

Dwight, Sally, Mark, and I spent most of Tuesday and Wednesday exploring various inland lakes on Drummond Island. By Thursday morning, there was only one lake left for us to explore, but it was difficult to get to from where we had camped at Marble Head, near the island's northeast corner. However, it was only about twelve miles away if we went by way of Lake Huron. And why not? Rather than arduously portaging our canoes through the woods all day—carrying them above our heads while we hiked—we could simply paddle up the shoreline on the edge of the big lake and arrive at our destination far less tired and in better time. The day was absolutely beautiful with not a cloud in the sky. We would soon learn that looks can be deceiving.

We woke up that morning and did our normal routine at the campsite. We ate breakfast around the campfire. Then we split up so we could each have our devotions—a quiet time meant for individual Bible reading and prayer. And then it was time to pack up camp for the day's adventures.

"I want to go rappelling," Dwight told the group. "How about we go back to that cliff?"

He was referring to a rock cliff we'd seen the day before. Dwight wanted to scout it as a possible site for taking campers. It would also be an opportunity to check our ropes and just make sure all of our equipment was in good working order. It wasn't a high cliff, maybe forty feet of rock face, but it was high enough for campers.

Dwight enjoyed rock climbing, belaying, and rappelling. As he said in his letter, "It never fails to amaze me how excited I am after climbing a cliff." Dwight was good at it, and he knew it was just the kind of activity that can help teens break out of their comfort zones and start to gain a new perspective on life. So, we headed out shortly after we cleaned up breakfast.

Now Dwight may have loved belaying and rappelling, but neither are really my personal favorite activity. Climbing a rock is one thing. You use all your God-given strength and skills to ascend a natural formation. But belaying and rappelling is something different. When you *rappel* a cliff or rock face, you use a system of ropes to descend to the ground. You put all of your trust in a relatively thin cable and a couple of gadgets designed to keep you from falling. *Belaying* is a name given to any number of techniques used to create friction on the rope itself, which of course will save your life if you're falling. If enough friction is created while you're falling, you'll come to a sudden, sharp stop in midair.

I wasn't interested in rappelling that morning. Instead, I planned to climb up to the top of the rock face, and then skirt down a hillside near the cliff. While Mark and Dwight got set up, Sally found a spot to sit in the sun. She was wearing shorts and a tank top and wanted to soak in as much of the rays as she could.

I started my climb up the rock face and was doing fine for the first few minutes. Dwight was holding the end of my line. Then I slipped on something and started to fall! Dwight was talking and didn't see me slip. When he noticed what was happening, he pulled the rope hard (belaying) which slammed me into the rock face!

"Dwight!" I yelled, allowing my annoyance to show for a minute. I'd fallen about fifteen feet before he stopped me. He probably saved me from having a broken leg or even worse. All the same, I got a cut on my left hand and a close encounter with a rock face that I hadn't wanted.

"Okay, that's it for me!" I yelled from the air. "My butt's too big to get up there. You guys can go ahead, but I'm coming back down." I rappelled back down the rock face—with Dwight paying close attention this time. We bandaged my hand and eventually laughed about it all. (I have a scar in that spot to this day.)

Eventually the guys were done, and it was time to get on with our trip up the shoreline. "I think you got sunburned, Sally," I said as we packed up. Her skin was clearly red across her legs and shoulders, but she didn't seem to mind.

By the time we made our way back to our campsite, it was time for lunch. The menu for this lunch included my favorites— peanut butter and jelly sandwiches, grapes, and gorp (trail mix that consists of nuts, M&M's, and pretzels—yummy). We chitchatted about our favorite music and bands that we each liked and played the game "name that tune in five bars." Sally won hands down as she was our talented musician! So, before setting out for Colton Bay, we ate our second meal of the day. We didn't know it at the time, but it was a good thing that rock climbing took as long as it did. The extra time allowed us to eat a second full meal before canoeing that day. We were going to need our strength.

～～～

Marble Head is an area that is mostly comprised of hiking trails and a few dirt roads. A scenic viewpoint on the shore called the Steps at Marble Head is one of the area's natural attractions. It is a structure of rocks that appear in a staircase-like fashion and is one hundred feet above the shoreline. The Steps at Marble Head and the viewpoint of the lake along the shore are among the island's highest, pristine, majestic places on the island.

Our plan was to paddle out of Marble Head into the edge of the North Channel, which is a smaller body of water that is part of Lake Huron. We would then follow the shoreline, paddling northwest along Drummond Island until we reached our destination.

The North Channel is about 160 miles long and is shaped something like a pea pod. The northern border is long and nearly flat. It hugs Ontario, Canada, with a shoreline that is populated by small marinas and picturesque coastal villages. The southern border of the channel is what curves down like a pea pod. A series of small Canadian islands separate the North Channel from the rest of Lake Huron, with Drummond Island in the leftmost corner of the channel.

Incidentally, we would travel right along the natural border between the United States and Canada. But our plan was to stick as close as we could to the shoreline of Drummond Island. There was no reason to venture into the big lake anyway. Our sights were set on the next inland lake, called Fourth Lake.

Before we left Marble Head we found a big wooden spool. It was just a couple of feet tall. Dwight wanted to take it back to Lake Ann because he thought it would make a cool nightstand. It was in decent shape, with just a little wear and tear, and Dwight liked it like that. That morning we tied the canoes side by side

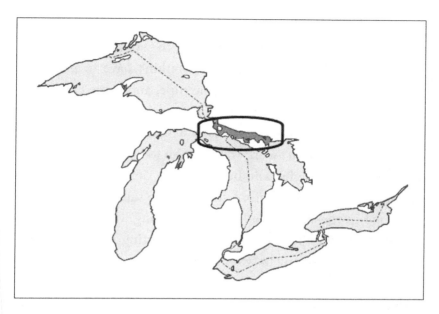

The North Channel of Lake Huron is a body of water directly east of Michigan's Upper Peninsula and bordered by several Canadian islands to the south and the Province of Ontario to the north.[2]

and put the spool in between us. It almost made our canoes feel like a pontoon.

Dwight and Sally got in one canoe, with Sally up front. I got in the other with Mark. Mark sat in the back of our canoe. Sally and Dwight led the way as we paddled into the small bay along the shore by the Marble Head viewpoint. It was an absolutely gorgeous day. We started canoeing northwest along the shoreline. We passed Sitgreaves Bay, Glen Point, and Glen Cove and paddled toward Sand Bay.

I'd never seen such rugged, absolutely gorgeous shoreline— with lush, green forests, sand and stone beaches, and luminous water. The beauty of God's creation was on display. The four of us were talking and having a great time in our pontoon-like canoes.

Dwight was always very adventurous. He decided it would be fun to create a makeshift sail, using the spool and a poncho. Dwight said, "If we had a sail, we wouldn't have to paddle so hard." Pulling out his poncho, some rope, and some carabiners, he managed to erect the "sail" between the four of us by balancing it in the spool. It actually worked for a little bit, too! But it ultimately didn't work well enough to keep it for very long. It started to get tangled and became more of a hassle. We ended up taking it down. But before doing so, the sail helped us notice a change in the wind. We kept on paddling. Our canoes were still tied together, and we were really starting to gain ground, working as a foursome in two linked canoes.

After a few miles I saw a dark cloud coming from the northwest, which was the direction we were headed. I thought, *Wow that's kind of dark, I wonder how far it is?* Well, we kept paddling and that thing started moving in. We talked about it but thought we would reach our destination before the storm arrived.

That's when I noticed the first sounds of *rustling*. It was almost like it was coming through the water. I could hear rustling in the trees too. Something about the wind was definitely changing and whatever it was, it was happening fast. The rustling seemed to be coming from everywhere. It was like Mother Nature was just about ready to get ticked off.

When we had first arrived on the island a few days prior, we checked the weather for the week while we were at the store in Drummond Township. It was supposed to be a clear week. There weren't any storm systems expected to arrive in the area until Friday afternoon or Friday night. But there was no mistaking what we could see up ahead. A storm was coming.

〰〰

If you've ever heard the term *freak storm*, well, I've actually seen one. They just seemed to appear out of nowhere. Clouds roll in and there is suddenly lightning, thunder, and heavy vertical wind and rainfall. I would learn later from a meteorologist that freak storms like the one that was headed for us appear once every ten to twelve years in the North Channel. The winds enter the channel from three different directions, creating a scenario for the "perfect" storms to appear suddenly, and then churn and rage without moving on. The winds seem to wrap themselves around the curve of the island. It only happens when the conditions are just right. We didn't know it at the time, but this would be one of those storms.

The fact that this storm was about to appear in a Great Lake was significant too. The Great Lakes are *huge* bodies of water. They are by far the largest freshwater lakes in the world.[3] When a storm appears on a Great Lake, the resulting waves can rival any waves you might find in ocean storms. Something that may seem surprising is that the Great Lakes can have undertows, similar to the ocean tides. This is especially true when storms and strong winds are churning the lake.

The storm was clearly coming in faster than our weather report had predicted. We felt the winds shift on the North Channel and we felt the temperature drop too. Typically, I love to take walks before storms. Even today, I'll see that a storm is coming and head out for a quick walk before the rain starts. I like to feel Mother Nature change her numerous moods.

I certainly remember feeling the change that day. The wind was getting colder. And it quickly became something we had to paddle against as it started to blow us back down the shoreline.

As the wind started to push and pull the canoes, the ropes tying them together became very tight and fighting the growing wind was increasingly difficult. We decided to untie the canoes so we could maneuver ourselves independently.

I remember looking up at the storm again and seeing that it was *much* closer.

Before we knew it, the wind was truly on top of us. It was cold and viscous. The canoes pushed and pulled against the ropes as the wind roared into their aluminum sides. At the same time, seemingly out of nowhere, a current just came to life on the lake and started dragging us—not back down the shoreline—but *away* from the shoreline.

At the same time, the heavens opened up and *buckets* of rain started falling. We could see lightning flashing in dark clouds overhead.

And then there were waves. Whitecaps, like you'd see on the ocean, started forming on Lake Huron. In a matter of minutes, the waves went from one to two feet high, to five to six feet high. They were just *crashing* over the sides of the canoes.

With the sudden rainfall and the crashing waves we were rapidly soaked head to toe and both canoes were taking on water. I had a big cup with me and started bailing water out of my canoe as quickly as I could. Sally was trying to do the same in her canoe while Mark and Dwight worked on the ropes.

Sally and I frantically switched from throwing water over the side to paddling as fast as we could toward Drummond Island. The problem was that even though we started just a few hundred feet from shore, we could not keep up with the enormous strength of the current. The storm was pulling us deeper into the North Channel than we ever intended to go.

This all happened so fast! We were completely surprised by the abruptness and intensity of this storm. One minute we were enjoying a scouting trip and the next we were fighting not to capsize into the frigid waters of Lake Huron. What had been a beautiful day filled with adventure and laughter had turned into an emergency situation.

The wind was violently smacking the aluminum canoes together. Then the current, or maybe a crosswind, would pull them apart, before the wind would smack them together again. It was *loud,* each hit was like a mini car accident with metal pounding against metal. Every lurch also poured more and more water into the canoes. Sally and I couldn't get the water out as fast as it was coming in. Dwight and Mark were still trying to get the ropes undone. We *had* to get those ropes untied. The water was really starting to swamp our canoes.

5

CAPSIZED!

It didn't take long before our canoes had taken on more water than they could handle. Dwight, Sally, Mark, and I began to sink. When aluminum canoes take on too much water they don't sink completely. Instead, they sit about six to twelve inches under the surface.

We capsized at about 2 p.m. that afternoon.[4] As we went down, Dwight closed his eyes and started to calmly pray, "Lord, we are in your hands. Help us with these elements, and the situation we are in." Even as he said these words our backpacks and supplies were being swept out into lake. Our walkie-talkies were lost and likely sinking to the bottom. The ropes that had tied us together were swept away.

As our canoes sunk and Dwight closed his eyes to pray, I remember thinking, *Lord, I'm not closing my eyes. I'm cinching this puppy up.* I pulled hard on my life jacket straps to make sure it was securely fastened.

Even though the situation was suddenly dire, I remember, the four of us did not panic. We had been trained in water safety and we were all believers. We trusted that God was in control of all things. Other than Dwight's prayer, the only other sound I remember hearing when we capsized was a loud, distinguishable gasp from the four of us as we each hit the water.

The water was so, so, freezing cold.

I looped my arm under the gunwale (the edge) of our submerged canoe. It may have been underwater, but it was something I could hold onto as I fought against the waves. The others did the same around their canoes.

One of the first things we tried to do was run one of the canoes over the other in order to get the water out. This means we attempted to push the submerged canoes against each other in the shape of a T, which would force one canoe to ride up on the gunwales of other one. This motion would push the top canoe up, out of the water. Once enough of the canoe was out of water, we could flip it by log rolling it back into the lake. In the process, most of the water would drain out. Ideally, when you run a canoe, you end up with at least one, mostly empty canoe. Then you run the second one up against the first and you'll have two seaworthy canoes again.

The four of us, treading frigid water and fighting waves, tried to run one canoe against the other. I was in the back, pushing the top canoe while Mark tried to steady it along the side. Dwight and Sally were on the other side of the submerged canoe, ready to grab the one I was pushing and then log roll it to dump out the water. With God as my witness, the *most enormous* winds came through just as we were doing this. They were just whipping around and *howling like a pack of wolves.* As soon as the wind got hold of the top canoe, that thing went flying through the air. I still remember it rolling up, and up into the wind. It was a ten-foot, sixty-pound aluminum canoe, but it was sent flying through the air like it was nothing. As if someone had flicked a giant toothpick into the winds, we watched that canoe go end over end through the air. One of our canoes was suddenly just suddenly *gone*.

The four of us were now desperately clinging to the one remaining canoe and shivering intensely against the frigid water. Dwight and I were on the right side of the canoe. He held onto the front while I held on near the back. Sally was on the left, up front next to Dwight, and Mark held onto the back left side, next to me. The waves were regularly cresting between three and six feet high. At this point we had just one oar left, which broke shortly afterward, and Mark tossed away because he realized he could paddle more easily without it. Everything else had been lost to the wind and waves.

We held onto the canoe by putting our elbows over the gunwale and pinching our bodies close to it. Then with our free arms we tried to paddle back toward the shore, but the current was way too strong. It was like we would paddle eight feet and then be thrown back nine. We worked and worked like this for at least an hour before we agreed to stop exhausting ourselves in futility. There was no way the four of us were strong enough to paddle to safety, and letting go of the canoe was not an option either, lest we be lost to the wind and waves like our other canoe was.

The current and the undertow immediately started pulling us out of Sand Bay and deeper into the North Channel itself. The police reports say we were only two hundred feet from shore, but I think it was much farther. The four of us debated about letting go of the now submerged canoe and swimming for the shore.

"I'm a good athlete," Mark said. "I think I can make it." Dwight thought about it for a few seconds, but said no.

"You need to stay with us," he said. "This is coming in way too fast. I don't think you'd make it to shore." Heeding his mentor's advice, Mark stayed with us and the canoe.

I would learn later that the water was just fifty-one degrees Fahrenheit that July third afternoon. All four of us were floating in it up to our chests with waves crashing over our heads and steady rain. We were shivering intensely and at a loss about what to do next. We were steadily being swept further out into the North Channel. Deeper into the storm.

HYPOTHERMIA

Drowning wasn't the greatest danger we were facing. All of us were strong swimmers. And all of us were wearing lifejackets. The danger we faced was hypothermia. The Centers for Disease Control and Prevention (CDC) describes hypothermia this way:

> Hypothermia is caused by prolonged exposures to very cold temperatures. When exposed to cold temperatures, your body begins to lose heat faster than it's produced. Lengthy exposures will eventually use up your body's stored energy, which leads to lower body temperature.
>
> Body temperature that is too low affects the brain, making the victim unable to think clearly or move well. This makes hypothermia especially dangerous, because a person may not know that it's happening and won't be able to do anything about it.
>
> While hypothermia is most likely at very cold temperatures, it can occur even at cool temperatures (above 40°F) if a person becomes chilled from rain, sweat, or submersion in cold water.[5]

We were in danger of hypothermia precisely because of that last line, "submersion in cold water." The lifejackets we had were the old-style, orange jackets that wrapped around your neck like a horseshoe and buckled in the front with white straps. They were not the vests you might picture a water skier wearing today, which wrap around your body and zipper up the front. These jackets helped us stay afloat as we fought the waves, but they did little to keep us warm. All of our vital organs were completely submerged in the frigid water. Even our arms were submerged as we clung to our just-under-the-surface canoe. The only things above water were our heads, but the storm still raged above us. The cold rain came down in sheets and the wind whipped past us, making it even colder.

On average, the interior temperature of the human body is about 98.6 degrees. You've probably experienced a fever before. When your body temperature is even just a handful of degrees too high—101 degrees or more—you end up flat on your back in bed, sick as a dog. Your health is at an even greater risk when your body temperature drops just a few degrees. Doctors recommend that if your temperature were to ever dip to 95 degrees Fahrenheit or lower—just 3.6 degrees lower than normal—you should immediately seek medical help. Hypothermia is therefore considered a medical emergency.

People suffering from hypothermia usually experience symptoms in stages. Symptoms don't all set in at once. They happen gradually, over time, as exposure to extreme cold is prolonged. The easiest way for me to explain it is with this scenario: In the first stage of hypothermia—if you have ever been outside playing in the snow for an extended amount of time and your boots and gloves get wet, then you've experienced this— you start shivering. If you stay in the elements and continue to get more clothing wet and stop shivering, you have just entered into the second stage. In the second stage of hypothermia, you will experience lack of coordination, slower breathing, a slower pulse, and sometimes a surge of warmth. What blood you had flowing into your extremities is moving toward your body's core to protect your vital organs.

If you do not get in quickly from the elements or get help, you will not realize that you have suddenly slipped into the third stage. In the third stage, if you are still outside and start to touch your arms and legs, they will feel like ice, and they will feel heavy. Confusion develops and you may hallucinate and talk of things that are not there (like a beach, sand, and the sun) but in your mind, you see them.

In the last stage of hypothermia, you feel extreme fatigue, soon a loss of consciousness, rigid limbs, and your pupils will totally dilate, then your body shuts down. Your body temperature has dropped too low and now you begin to slip into death. That is why hypothermia is called a "silent killer."

FLOATING

Floating there, clinging to our submerged canoes as we were pulled farther and farther away from Drummond Island, I saw the concern in Dwight's face. Due to our survival training, we both fully understood the danger we were in—not only from our capsized situation, but especially from hypothermia. That concern, however, never became hysteria on any of our parts.

The Mayo Clinic adds the following on their webpage about hypothermia: "The confused thinking associated with hypothermia prevents self-awareness. The confused thinking can also lead to risk-taking behavior."[6]

The four of us focused on trusting in our Lord and Savior as the daylight hours passed into night. We had no way of knowing how or when we'd be dry and warm again. But with our vital organs submerged in frigid water, we knew it wouldn't be long before the effects of hypothermia started to set in.

THE LONG NIGHT

Due to the unique nature of the North Channel, these freak storms tend to camp out in one location without much movement. I would learn later that the storm stayed in place for about ten hours, surging and abating and surging again. We didn't know what was happening at the time. Since we had been pulled deep into the channel, our only option seemed to be to wait out the storm.

Over the years I've had people ask me, "what did you do all night?" Well, we all tried to keep moving, kicking our legs together like a lifeguard doing "scissor kicks" up to try and get some of our body out of the water for a brief time. Through the constant battering of the storm, and in the deep darkness, we just tried to console each other in prayer and song. We sang a number of hymns that night. I specifically remember singing, "Amazing Grace," "Jesus, Hold My Hand," and "I'll Fly Away." All of us were fans of Amy Grant too and so we sang her song, "My Father's Eyes." This song has especially poignant lyrics, considering our surroundings that night:

> She had her Father's Eyes . . .
> Eyes that found the good in things
> When good was not around
> Eyes that found the source of help
> When help would not be found.

We also talked about our families, wanting to see them again, and other loved ones.

Many times, we just talked to God.

Off and on that night, depending upon the waves and the clouds, we could barely make out a light flashing on another shore. We thought it was a lighthouse. Dwight said to me and the others, "If we make it to that shore, go south. Try to find the lighthouse." But then the storm would kick up again and we would fight to stay above water, losing any sense of where the shore was.

That night I made sure that I was right with the Lord. We could all feel that we were still drifting further and further into the North Channel, and we knew that if God did not send us a boat, well, we tried not to think that way, and kept up hope.

I'd been a student at a couple of different Christian schools. I knew young people that did what I call "playing the game." They talk the talk of a Christian, but they don't walk the walk. I'm a sinner just like everyone else, so that night, in the dark and the cold I made sure that I was in good standing with my Creator. If I didn't make it through this night on Lake Huron, I wanted to be ready to meet Jesus.

THE SILENT KILLER

As the storm raged and faded and raged again, we were pulled farther away from Drummond and pushed closer to Cockburn Island, a small island that is part of Canada. The distance between Drummond Island and Cockburn Island is only 18.2 miles. The channel that runs between them is called the False Detour Channel. It's also a small, natural water boundary between the U.S. and Canada.

I look back at that night and I remember it being very, very violent. I never took the official lifeguard test, but I did do the training. I learned that seventy percent of the body heat we lose comes off our heads. So, every time a wave would slam against the canoe, we would have to scissor kick to get up out of the water. We tried everything we could to keep our heads up and out of the lake. But of course, we all got slammed into the canoe many times because we wouldn't see a wave coming behind us. It was nearly pitch dark sometimes and the waves were moving in a violent, erratic fashion. It was also raining off and on all night long.

Dwight, Sally, Mark, and I just kept getting slammed on either side. But we made every effort to keep moving. If you stopped moving, you'd freeze to death.

SALLY COON

Some of the lyrics to the hymn "I'll Fly Away" go like this:

> *Some glad mornin' when this life is over*
> *I'll fly away*
> *To a home on God's celestial shore*
> *I'll fly away*

During the night—I'm guessing now around 10:30 or 11 p.m.—I noticed that Sally wasn't moving a lot. It was actually her hair that tipped me off.

Sally had long, pretty, blond hair. From my position at the back right of the canoe, I could see the back of Sally's head as she was holding onto the canoe diagonally from me, along the front left. All afternoon and into the evening, the four of us struggled and kicked against the storm. While we did this, I saw Sally's long hair moving in the water. Each time she scissor-kicked up, it moved with her, fanning out in the water behind her shoulders. Each time a wave came crashing onto her head, it was tossed wildly. And so, I noticed when her hair wasn't moving as much anymore.

The storm was ebbing and not as strong as it had been earlier in the day. The sun had gone down, and a deep darkness and cold had set in. With the canoe being submerged a good six inches, Sally and I were able only to keep our heads above water most of the time. Sometimes the guys could get up a little higher than we could, but by that time of night all of us were tired and even they were only able to keep their heads above water.

I tried to move as much as I could in order to stay warm. We'd been in the frigid water now for somewhere between eight and nine hours. It was so dark that night. The moon was just a sliver, and you could see a glimpse of its light settled behind the clouds. Sometimes, with the position of the clouds, it was hard to see even Dwight, who was just a few feet in front of me on the right side of the canoe. As the clouds moved through the sky that early July fourth morning, you would briefly see a little more sliver of the moon's light reflect through the clouds and onto the surface of the water. And that was a welcome sight to see, but not for long did it stay.

All of us were getting tired. While we tried to talk to each other during the storm, we hadn't been talking as much after the sun went down.

Yet, even in the dark I noticed that Sally's hair just wasn't moving that much, which meant *she* wasn't moving that much.

Another sign that something was wrong was that Sally had stopped shivering. She had been shivering all afternoon and evening as we fought the storm—we all were. It was an obvious change. I knew at that time Sally was suffering the effects of hypothermia more than the rest of us.

Was she starting to feel warm? Confused? Were the late-stage effects of the silent killer setting in? Had her sunburn from earlier in the day made it worse? Had her skinned cooled more quickly than the rest of us because of the burn?

And then I remember that Sally just let go. Mark, who was clutching the canoe behind her, was kind of in a daze.

"Mark!" I screamed to get his attention. "*Sally!*"

Mark let go of the canoe and took a few strokes out into the darkness, but he couldn't find her. She never made a sound. The current just seemed to pull her away. She was just gone, just like that. All of a sudden, just gone from us.

In order to stabilize the canoe, I moved to the back left side, where Mark had been.

"Cheryl, I can't see her! I can't find her!" Mark said. Mark swam back to the canoe and we both kept yelling for her. "Sally! Sally! We are over here! Sally!"

We never heard a sound from Sally. Looking back, I think she was probably in one of the final phases of hypothermia and a strong wave or undertow likely lifted her elbow out of the submerged canoe and just pulled her away. It was an eerie feeling.

Mark and I kept on yelling for her, hoping for a response. That's when I noticed a conspicuous quiet from Dwight.

If Dwight yelled for Sally that night, I don't remember it. I remember Mark and I yelling, but not Dwight. I don't know if Dwight truly understood what was going on at the time. When Mark returned to the canoe, I moved back to my spot behind Dwight. I remember that he looked over at us with an expression like, "where is she?" but I cannot be sure he was coherent enough to have said anything.

Looking back, I believe that if Dwight had been in his right mind, he would have taken off after Sally like Mark did. But at the moment, I wasn't connecting those dots. I was just praying and holding out hope that Sally would make it to shore or that God would soon send a late-night fisherman or boater to find her and us.

DWIGHT HERZBERGER

Shortly thereafter, maybe just twenty minutes or so, Dwight also began to physically show signs of succumbing to the cold. He had turned around in the water to face me and started talking. It was like he wasn't there with us in Lake Huron. He was talking about something that happened in the past. He was mumbling about a beach.

"I got to get to the beach," he said. "Are we going to the beach?"

Then he turned back around and fell silent.

"Cheryl, I'm worried about him," Mark said.

"Hey, Dwight!" I spoke into the darkness. "Stay awake. Talk to us." He turned around again and talked a little bit, but nothing made sense of what he said. Then he turned back toward the front. He did this back and forth a few times and sometimes just lay against the canoe.

I swam up to him at the front of the canoe and realized he'd stopped shivering.

Lord, have mercy! I prayed. We had to act fast.

"Mark, let's get him into the canoe."

Getting Dwight into the canoe was not an easy task. While there was a break in the storm, it hadn't gone completely out of the channel. Mark and I were also still battling the undertow. Meanwhile, Dwight wasn't fighting us, but he wasn't helping us either.

I lifted his legs on the right side of the canoe while Mark pulled on his body from the opposite side. We had to be careful to keep the canoe stable while we pulled him in, lest we roll it and allow it to get sucked away by an undertow.

We somehow managed to pull Dwight into the still-submerged canoe.

"Dwight," I said, "now sit in there. Sit down."

I directed him to a pair of two-by-fours that had been wedged into the middle of the canoe to fashion an extra seat for campers. The canoes were designed with only one metal seat in the front and another in the back. So, we often added two-by-fours to the middle to make an extra seat.

Dwight sat on that wooden seat. I kept talking to him. I remember that he was dressed that day as he almost always was—in shorts, boots, and a T-shirt—and of course the orange life jacket.

I patted him on the leg. "Stay with us, Dwight. Talk to me, buddy."

He tried to respond, but it was already too late. He became increasingly incoherent, and he kept trying to stand up. Mark and I didn't want him to stand because he could easily lose his balance and roll the canoe, or he might fall in and be lost as quickly as Sally was.

Dwight managed to get into a half-kneeling position. He seemed so confused or disoriented and I could just tell he'd entered another stage of hypothermia.

He was kind of talking incoherently. He honestly could've been at Myrtle Beach in his mind—a place he loved. But then all of a sudden he stopped mumbling. He just stood up as best he could and dove to the left side, out of the canoe, and swam away. I could hear him going at the water. Though Dwight was surely in the later stages of hypothermia at that point, he still had a little bit of energy, because he swam away from us quickly.

Mark tried to grab him, but Dwight was gone from the canoe. Mark swam after him, but it was so dark he couldn't see him anywhere. "DWIGHT! DWIGHT!" We yelled and yelled, but soon the rustling of the water stopped. Dwight had drifted away from us into the darkness.

A DECISION TO MAKE

T he sun had gone down that night around 9:30 p.m. By the time both Sally and Dwight left us, it was most likely near or after midnight. We tried and tried to find them and yell for them, but we couldn't see anything, nor did we hear any response.

It was so dark and so immensely cold. We continued drifting farther away from Drummond Island. We were being pushed along the southern edge of the North Channel and toward Cockburn Island. It was hour after hour of scissor kicking up out of the waves while we clutched the edge of a freezing aluminum canoe. We didn't dare conserve our energy—we really couldn't have—because we would've frozen to death.

Around 3 a.m., it was finally still. The lake was like glass. I remember looking up and thinking that it looked gorgeous. The sky was different too. The clouds had been so dark. But at that time, they turned to a dark streak of gray. It was like you could reach up and touch them. I could finally see a little more of the sky than just the North Star, too. We couldn't see much past the clouds, but the North Star was beautiful. Gorgeous.

The storm had a lot of facets. When the storm went through, it felt like fury. Then it was like the storm got to thinking, pondering, and the fury would ebb a little bit. Then it would get furious again and the wind and waves would rage.

At some point when the storm was quiet, I fell asleep, elbow and head against the canoe. I had entered the next stage of hypothermia and the silent killer was coming for me. While I was sleeping, Mark kicked the canoe. I don't know if he jerked involuntarily, or what exactly happened but my head slammed against the canoe very hard, and it cut me. I woke up and felt blood on the left side of my forehead. I looked over at Mark to find out what had happened.

"Oh, Lord Jesus!" I whispered and began frantically swimming toward him.

Mark's head was tilted with one ear submerged in the water. He was still alive, but whatever state he was in, he was unable to keep his own head up.

"Mark! Mark! Are you alright?" He didn't respond. I knew I had to do something to get his head up quickly.

I started to move him. The water was finally calm enough to attempt something like this. It was as flat as could be. Dark and cloudy still, but at least the waves and rain had finally stopped. After a great struggle of effort, I finally got him into the canoe and somehow managed to avoid rolling it under the surface. I knew I needed to talk to Mark. I had to keep him awake and try somehow to keep him warm. The final stages of hypothermia were clearly setting in.

"Don't you let go!" I said to him. "We've got to make it! We've got to get some help!" In a moment of frustration, I could've shaken him. But I knew at that time that what I really needed to do was get him out of the water.

I thought if I could get into the canoe too, then I could do a better job of taking care of Mark. But I was afraid that climbing into the canoe would upset it and dump him back into the lake. So I decided to lean over the side of the canoe and do what I could from there. I leaned over as far as I could with my five-foot-four stature and started rubbing Mark's arms and legs in an attempt to warm him. I also kept talking to him. I don't know how long I did this. And I didn't know it at the time, but I was adding more injury to my already injured body by leaning against the side of the canoe for so long.

It eventually just got so that I was *so cold*. I *had* to get into the canoe and try to warm myself and Mark.

I don't know how but by the grace of God, I maneuvered myself into the canoe without tipping it, which would have thrown Mark and myself splashing into the water. I have often thought back to that night and am amazed—I still do not know how that canoe did not tip over and roll! I honestly think there were angels there that night, something besides me that held the canoe upright.

I sat down in the center of the canoe. I was still submerged under the waterline by a few inches. Mark and I were still waist deep in frigid water even in the canoe. But at least the storm had finally relented to calmness. At least we didn't have to keep treading water and scissor-kicking our bodies above the waves.

I pulled Mark's muscular, athletic body toward me. It wasn't easy. I pulled him right up against me with his hip toward my torso. I tried to keep the canoe from rolling by pressing my legs as hard as I could into either side of the canoe. Keeping my feet separated was a way of distributing weight to both sides of the canoe, and hopefully it would keep us from rolling. I positioned his head on my left forearm and supported his head and neck into the crest of my elbow.

Mark was in a bad way. But at least in this position, with him lying on his side up against me, we could share what little body heat we had left and I could see his face, which was inches away, and he could see mine.

"Now don't go anywhere, Mark," I demanded. "You need to stay right here with me. Mark, you hear me?"

"Cheryl, we're not going to make it," he said. "I'm not going to make it."

"Mark, you've got to stay with me." I frantically rubbed his arms and legs as I spoke. "We're almost to Cockburn. We've got to swim for it."

"I don't know if I can. I'm tired. I'm real tired."

I probably rubbed Mark's arms and legs for more than an hour, it seemed. I was so close to Mark's chiseled face that as the clouds shifted and slivers of moonlight were cast downward, I could see that both of his eyes were becoming totally dilated. And while he was responding to me at first, eventually he stopped talking.

At this point, it was probably around 4:30 a.m. I could make out the horizon and the dark island some distance away—a thin line in the darkness—but the sun wasn't up yet. I was praying over and over for a fisherman or boats. I thought maybe there was a chance that some early bird might be out and maybe, with God's help, they might see us.

In an effort to keep Mark awake and warm, I pulled him up higher against me. I was able to carefully get his head up from the crook of my elbow and almost on top of my left shoulder. We were still in the middle of the canoe, more toward the back than the front.

Would anyone see us? Would God send a fisherman? Did Dwight and Sally make it to shore? I just kept praying.

MARK TAUBE

I had been rubbing Mark's hands and arms with my right hand. I would also take my hand and periodically pass over his nose and mouth to feel his breath. I don't know exactly how fast it happened, a matter of seconds or a minute, but Mark stopped breathing. He hadn't spoken in a long time. He hadn't moved of his own accord and his eyes had fully dilated. His eyes were entirely black pupils! (I could see that now, as the sliver of light on shore rose more on the horizon.)

"Oh, no! Mark!"

I grabbed his shoulders and pulled him up. I pinched his nose and performed mouth-to-mouth resuscitation. I gave him three breaths, stopped, checked his breath, but couldn't hear anything. I wanted to try CPR but I couldn't get into a position to do the chest compressions in the tipsy, submerged canoe. You need a solid surface.

"Please help me, God!" I pleaded out loud. "Please help, Jesus!"

I gave Mark three more breaths. Mark coughed, but I could hear the gurgle of water. He breathed again. It was very shallow breathing that lasted about two or three minutes. Just right there in the elbow of my arm, hugging him close with my other arm, Mark took his last breath on this earth and died.

When it all happened it seemed very fast, but now looking back, it feels like an eternity. The storm had finally subsided, but Mark was gone. When I think back to that night of my life,

I honestly believe that if Mark Taube hadn't woken me up by kicking the canoe, then I wouldn't be alive today. We would've both died in the water. God used him (and the blunt edge of the canoe) to literally knock me upside the head and pull me out of the silent killer's sleep. It was life-changing to experience such a tragic moment. But in some odd sense it was also a blessing—a blessing to have been with my friend Mark during the last moments of his earthly life.

What happened in the next minute is hard to describe. I couldn't see much of anything. It was still dark. I looked to the horizon out in front of us and could make out the North Star in a break in the clouds, and I thought maybe I'd seen a light flashing on the shore of Cockburn Island, but other than that, I was just floating in the dark alone in Lake Huron. That's when I felt it, a sensation that just happened right there, Mark's soul ascended to heaven. I felt this warmth move right past my chest and just ASCEND, ASCEND UPWARD! I held him close and remember tilting my head and looking up and saying, "Lord, welcome Mark into your Heaven because he just stood in front of Jesus."

I didn't *see* anything that night. But out there in the middle of Lake Huron, in forty-nine-degree water, where I'd been since roughly 2 p.m. the previous day—fourteen hours—I felt an undeniable warmth leave Mark and move past me. I believe God gives us, all of us, a soul. And I knew that something had brushed me that night in the canoe and had risen upward.

When Mark left, I felt an immediate loneliness I had not felt up to that point. I knew Mark had passed. I felt his soul go past me, and I was alone, still sitting in a submerged canoe, freezing, weak, bleeding, and holding onto Mark's body.

But I never gave up. Maybe Dwight or Sally made it. Maybe an early morning fisherman would see me. I put my trust in God and just kept praying. I just kept asking God to help.

I also continued to try and keep Mark's head out of the water. This was hard to do because the canoe was fully submerged along with the weight of our two bodies. It may have been supporting us, but our heads and shoulders were still very close to the waterline.

I had read that if someone had low body temperature, it might be possible to revive them if they could just warm up. It was strange. I knew Mark had passed. I had felt it. Yet, I just wanted to keep his head above the water.

The sliver of light on the horizon had begun to shine brighter. The island's shoreline was starting to appear, and I knew dawn was approaching. I don't know exactly how long I sat like this, praying and trying to keep Mark above water. Five minutes? Ten minutes? Fifteen? I'm not sure. But I remember that eventually I looked at my own fingernails and saw another sign of hypothermia. They were *so* white. This is one of the things that happens during hypothermia. Blood rushes to the core, to the vital organs, while extremities—like fingers—change color because they have lost so much of their internal heat.

I knew that I had a decision to make. I could stay in that canoe with Mark's body, and hope and pray that someone would find us. Or I could try and swim for shore. But what about Dwight and Sally? I still held out hope that I would see them again. Would it be better to stay in the canoe and try to find them?

But I also knew I was freezing to death. Eventually, I honestly thought, *Do I stay in this canoe and die, or do I swim for it and try to make it or die trying?*

So I eased myself out of the canoe, trying not to rock it too much. I tried to pull Mark up out of the water as best I could. I said goodbye to Mark's body and swam into the darkness toward the island.

LANDING

The sun did not come up that day until a little before 6 a.m. I swam through the frigid waters as dawn slowly approached. I saw the outline of the shore of Cockburn Island a mile or so away. Then I got a horrific cramp in my left leg. A charley horse like I'd never felt before.

On my back, trying to stretch that horrific charley horse out, I said out loud, "Lord, Please *help*, get me to that island and I promise I will eat a banana every day." (Potassium is my friend!) I did the backstroke and just kept moving and praying.

Finally, after swimming for a mile or more, I stumbled onto the jagged, rocky shore, falling multiple times as I tried to gain my footing. If I would have been boating at that time and noticed me on the shore, I would have looked like I was totally drunk! When I could finally stand without falling over, I looked down at myself and saw blood all over me from various cuts and scrapes. I must have looked horrid.

But even in this state, God showed me something beautiful. That morning on Cockburn Island I saw the prettiest sunrise I'd ever seen in my life. It was incredible. Not a cloud in the sky on July 4.

I also knew that I *had* to keep walking. My training told me that I was still in danger of hypothermia. If I would have sat down and rested, I almost certainly would've died from the cold. I had to get my core warmed up. I decided to look for the lighthouse and started walking along the shore toward the spot I'd last seen from the water's perspective.

The "lighthouse" we thought we'd seen that night was actually just a big, long electrical box alongside the back of the shore. I climbed up on the top and pushed open the lid. I had read that sometimes on small islands, with this type of warning for boats and ships, there is a switch inside the box to turn the lights on manually. I thought to myself, *If I can flip that switch, maybe someone will think it is odd to have the light on during the day and come and investigate.* So, I thought about it for a few seconds as I surveyed the box.

God blessed me with a wicked sense of humor. I looked down into that box and saw *water* surrounding all the electronics. I had just survived a full night in a freezing lake. I was not about to be electrocuted! All I could think was, *I would be dead, but I'd have a great perm at my funeral!* I decided to jump down and keep walking.

The sun was up by that time and shining brightly. The sun's warmth that radiant July morning truly saved me from freezing to death! Even though I was out of the water, my core temperature had dropped critically low. I knew I needed to keep moving in order to bring my vital organs back up to a safe temperature.

If it had been a little bit hazy or cloudy on that Independence Day morning, or if there had been rain coming down, then I wouldn't be alive today. Doctors confirmed this for me after the fact. I was in desperate need for an external source of heat–the sun.

I walked up the shore quite a ways, feeling the sun on my back and on my head, slowly getting me warmer. I didn't see anyone, but I thought I heard the sound of cars, and so I headed off the shore and into the woods. I walked for hours continually active, warmed by the sun throughout parts of the woods. I thought I heard cars but never found them; neither did I find a road or any signs of human life. After a while I was finally warm and took off my old orange life jacket.

Roughly five and a half hours later, I came smack-dab down the hill out of the woods and onto the shore again. Straight out in the water in front of me, I could see the canoe with Mark's body still floating in it. I had done a one-hundred-eighty-degree turn! After hours of walking, I was still alone and right back where I'd started.

HELP ARRIVES

A couple of sail boats went by, but I couldn't get their attention. They were too far away from the island. I had nothing left at this point, so I just sat down on the shore and said out loud, "Lord, I am worn out, *exhausted*. I have no idea what to do next. Please help me to get some help now." A few seconds passed by and God responded. I heard an engine. It was a boat!

Now, talk about being ironic. After a long night spent submerged in freezing lake water and a five-and-a-half-hour walk around the woods, I could see a huge boat just offshore that could help me—but I couldn't get the driver's attention! I was shouting and waving, but he couldn't hear me. Finally, he spotted the canoe and Mark's body and cut his engines.

He finally spotted me, but he wasn't bringing the boat near. It was a small yacht. The two people aboard were a middle-aged couple from Flint, Michigan, obviously out for a pleasure cruise on a holiday weekend. The sun was brilliant, and the lake was beautiful, giving no hint of the fury of the storm from the previous night.

"Hey! Hey! Help, help!" I just kept yelling. He finally yelled back. I told him to radio the United States Coast Guard, as I had two other friends that were missing, and I did not know if they had been rescued or what happened. I saw him pick up his radio and relay the message for help. Then he yelled back, "Young lady, I just recently bought this boat! That shoreline is *really* rocky. I don't want to scratch up the bottom of the hull. Could you swim out to me?"

I kid you not! Have you ever been watching a movie, and someone says something that just stops you short? You think, *did he just say that? Really?* Well, that's what this moment felt like. Did he really just ask me to get back *into* the frigid water?

Well, yes, he did! I look back on this moment and I think if God had not given me a sense of humor, I honestly do not know how I would have made it through this life. Life is just too short and too fragile. You have to laugh. You have to have that sense of humor and realize that the place you're in is not the place you're always going to be in.

I don't think I actually laughed that morning, but I strapped my lifejacket back on and said, "OK, here we go again, Lord." Then I once again entered the freezing water of Lake Huron and started swimming for my life.

PART III

AFTERMATH
of GRACE

MEDICAL MIRACLE

The kind, middle-aged couple in the yacht had to physically pull me on board. All my remaining strength was gone. I had made the swim out to their boat, but I couldn't even climb up without help. The man came down to the lowest part of the yacht's deck. He and his wife worked together to lift my 140 pounds up out of the water.

She immediately sat me down, gave me a blanket and water to drink while he contacted the authorities. They introduced themselves and told me they were from Flint. I talked rapidly and told them the situation as they listened with intent. They reached both the US Coast Guard as well as the Canadian Mountie Police. (We had crossed into international waters between the US and Canada). While we waited for them to arrive, the man slowly circled the area. About six hundred yards away, he spotted two objects in the water, and as the man slowly drove his yacht closer, I could see Sally and Dwight's bodies not very far from each other, floating face down in the water. That is when it really hit me like a ton of bricks. Right in that moment I knew that they did not make it. For the first time during the whole ordeal, I allowed myself to really cry.

Just twenty-four hours before, Dwight, Sally, Mark, and I were having lunch at Marble Head, talking and laughing—having a great time. Then, in such a short time, I'd survived the worst storm I've ever seen in my life, but three of my friends did not. How could this have happened?

> I don't know what time it was exactly when Sally drifted away, or when Dwight left us. Was it late on July 3? Or during the wee hours of July 4? I don't know if it was technically "morning" or not, but I'll tell you one thing I do know: because of my confidence in the promises of God, because I know Dwight, Sally, and Mark had all placed their faith in him, I know without a doubt, that when they opened their eyes next on that "glad morning" they were truly on "God's celestial shore." Their bodies may have been left somewhere in Lake Huron, but their souls were with God.
>
> For God so loved the world that he gave his one and only Son, that whoever believes in him shall not perish but have eternal life. For God did not send his Son into the world to condemn the world, but to save the world through him. Whoever believes in him is not condemned, but whoever does not believe stands condemned already because they have not believed in the name of God's one and only Son. (John 3:16–18)

In addition to my emotions coming to the surface, I started to become aware of the physical trauma I'd endured. Everything hurt. I had absolutely no strength left. I had been so cold, for so long, only to regain some of my heat while walking for five and half hours (without food), and then to lose much of that heat again with the swim out to the yacht. I was completely worn out, totally exhausted. I would learn later that my muscles were literally breaking down at this point. Not only was my body fighting to stay warm, not only was I cut and bruised everywhere, but my muscle tissue was literally falling apart on me. I was saved at last, but I felt totally spent.

MEDICAL MIRACLE OR HOSPITAL SIDESHOW?

After all the authorities arrived, there was a short debate about who was going to retrieve and care for the bodies of Dwight, Sally, and Mark. Would it be the Canadian Mounties or the US Coast Guard? As I listened to them go back and forth I started to get bothered. These were my friends. I just wanted them out of the water! I put my life jacket back on and thought, *If you can't get them out, then I will. I'm going to jump in there myself and get them.* So, what adrenaline I had left kicked in and I walked to the back of the yacht, ready to dive in. Just then the lady put her hand on my shoulder and gently pushed me to the seat. She turned and yelled, "You men get her friends' bodies out of this water right now! My husband and I will take Cheryl into the dock near the hospital, now radio the ambulance to meet us there!"

The Flint couple took me to the dock while the authorities settled their plans and retrieved the bodies. EMTs were waiting for me. They brought a gurney right onto the boat. I remember the loud clank of the gurney wheels hitting the deck of the yacht.

The EMTs had me lie down and strapped me in. They fastened a blood pressure cuff on me and checked my blood pressure several times. They also used a stethoscope to check my respiration and shined a light in my pupils. I am guessing they were looking to see if my body was going into shock after all it had been through. With their initial exams complete, the EMTs lifted the gurney up onto the dock and started pushing me toward a waiting ambulance.

I would learn later that the Canadian Mountie Police had arranged for the ambulance to be waiting at the dock. I would also learn later that while the Flint couple drove me to the dock, both the Canadian Mountie police and the US Coast Guard stayed to retrieve the bodies of Dwight, Sally, and Mark.

At the time of these events, everything seemed liked it was moving in slow motion. I remember that the dock was long and wooden. I remember the sound of the gurney's wheels—plunk, plunk, plunk—echoing loudly as they crossed each wooden plank on that dock. The thoughtful EMTs rolled the gurney slowly across those bumpy planks to avoid jarring me too much.

I fell asleep soon after I was loaded into the ambulance because of exhaustion. I woke up when they took me out of the ambulance. I remember being pushed through the emergency room doors of a small hospital. They had moved me to the far northeastern side of Manitoulin Island. Like Cockburn Island, Manitoulin Island is technically part of the province of Ontario, Canada. I was in a little town called Little Current. While this was happening, authorities radioed the camp and notified Eldon Brock of the tragedy. My parents were also notified.

After my arrival at this small-town hospital, I quickly became a "medical miracle." I was alive, but with no reasonable, scientific explanation for it. I was reminded that the average life expectancy for surviving water that cold is between three to five hours. They estimated that I had spent approximately 15 HOURS in lake water that was a mere 49 to 50 DEGREES! I then swam a mile or more to Cockburn Island. Then I walked aimlessly for another five and a half hours after reaching shore.

This information astounded the nursing staff and the doctors. What I had endured was considered much more than the human body should have been able to withstand. Frankly, the fact that I hadn't fallen over dead on the island astounded everyone who was treating me. I started to hear voices talking behind the curtains, medical personnel.

"That's the one . . ."

"That's her?"

"She's the one who lasted 15 HOURS in the waters of Lake Huron . . ."

"Unbelievable . . ."

It didn't take long for this "medical miracle" to start to feel more like a hospital side show.

Adding to the spectacle, I was cut and bruised all over. My hands had cuts from gripping the metal sides of the canoe, some of which were sharp. My forearms, legs, and torso were all bruised from being slammed against the canoe in the waves. My ribs were particularly bruised from all the hours leaning over the aluminum side of the canoe in order to stay afloat and while I was rubbing Mark's arms and legs and talking with him. I had a cut on the upper left side of my forehead from where I slammed into the canoe after I'd fallen asleep.

At 5:45 that evening I gave an official statement which was later typed.

Weeks later, back at home, a friend would say to me, "Cheryl, you looked awful. Like you had been in the ring with a heavyweight boxer for a couple of rounds." You look like you

Statement of:-   Taken at:-Little Current Hospital

Cheryl Steele   Date: 4th JULY 1980

Melvindale, Michigan   At: 1745 Hr.

Mark TAUBE, Dwight HERZBERGER, Sally COON and I were staff members of
the Regular Baptist Camp of Michigan located at Lake Ann, Michigan.
We were on a survey trip to locate camp sites for future trips.
We arrived at Drummond Island on Tuesday evening to begin a survey
of the area. On Thursday 03 JULY 80 about noon we left the area known
as Marblehead by canoe and were heading across the bay near the mouth
for Glen Cove. I was in one canoe with Mark TAUBE and Dwight and
Sally were in the other canoe. Before we left, we tied the two
canoes together side by side. The wind was at our back and we used
a poncho to fashion a makeshift sail. We had gone about two miles
when the wind changed and began blowing us back the way we had
come. It became much stronger, we took down our sail and started
paddling. We were about one mile from shore when both canoes filled
with water and submerged. We clung to the canoes and kicked and
stroked toward the nearest land on Drummond Island. We were about
two hundred feet from calm water when the wind shifted again and
seemed to strengthen. We were unable to make any headway and were
being blown toward Cockburn Island. By this time the sun was going
down and we decided to go with the wind. Shortly after the canoes
had filled with water the canoes had just about come apart. Mark
cut one loose and we clung to the other one. About three hours after
dark Sally drifted away from the canoe. Mark grabbed her but he

*Page one of a two-page statement given to Canadian authorities
on July 4, 1980.*

were almost beat to death! I was black and blue all over my body. In addition to what could be seen on the outside, I had liver damage from leaning over the side of the canoe so much.

I remember the officer from the Ontario Provincial Police who was in charge of the investigation and who took my statement at the Little Current hospital. I don't remember his name or what his exact title and rank was. I only remember that he was so, so nice. He was probably in his forties, and I know he had a couple of young kids.

The officer's wife was there too, and she ended up giving me her clothes to wear. As strange as it sounds, I needed clothes! At some point, when I was brought into the hospital, totally exhausted, black and blue, and in danger of hypothermia, someone snipped off most of my clothes in order to begin treatment on my body. So, this officer's wife gave me some of hers. I remember her slowing and carefully walking me to his car before they took me from the Little Current hospital to the airport on Manitoulin, where I would meet my flight back to Michigan.

BACK IN THE USA

I was flown back to the United States by a little, twin-engine plane. Eldon Brock chartered the flight. He and his wife, Trudy, flew over to Manitoulin to meet me at the hospital and bring me home. We left Little Current on a sunny early Saturday afternoon (July 5) and flew into the city of Alpena, on Michigan's northeast side, for processing at US Customs. We then flew straight on to Traverse City. We had no problems or delays in Customs at all. I think all the employees had heard the amazing story and knew I was arriving.

Eldon had coordinated with my family to meet us at the Cherry Capital Airport in Traverse City. My niece Kelley had been a camper that week. So, when I exited the twin-engine plane in Traverse City, I was greeted by my mom, my sister Carolyn, and Kelley. (My dad stayed back at my family home and waited for me there, as he was unable to make the trip due to complications with his health.) I remember my mom crying and hugging me so tight that I had to tell her, "Please ease up, mom. That hurts." Immediately, she looked at my bruises and turned her head from me. She didn't want me to see her aghast look and tried to hide her expressions. My family took me straight over to Munson Medical Center in Traverse City. Later, Carolyn and Kelley went back to the camp that Saturday evening to stay.

Everything hurt. The extent of my injuries was still being discovered and they were afraid my body was going to slip into a state of shock. At one point, the staff at Munson had me try to squeeze vice grips in my hand to measure my strength. I couldn't budge them. I'd lost a lot of muscle over the long night of treading water on Lake Huron. Everything in me hurt. My ribs in particular were incredibly sore. We thought at one point that I must've broken some, but it turned out to be severe bruising from the canoe.

I remember lying quietly on a gurney late that morning. My mother was sitting in a chair nearby, while the rest of my family was waiting back at the camp. A few nurses were milling about the room, getting things set up. Some were still chitchatting in the hallway nearby about me, the "medical miracle."

Then, to my complete surprise, in walked a drop-dead-gorgeous doctor. As it turned out, he would be my treating physician. I was fine with that! I remember he had deep, beautiful blue eyes and amazing hair. I'm not kidding. Back then we would've called him "Mr. Dreamy." This guy was extremely good looking! I thought to myself, *Yes, I'm alive! I'm alive! (And you are gorgeous.)*

The doctor had my chart, looked down at it, and after a minute said rather loudly, "What the hell?!"

All the nurses suddenly got quiet.

"Young lady, do you know you were in Lake Huron for—are you kidding me—fifteen hours?!" The handsome doctor started pacing back and forth with my chart attached to the clipboard. "Fifteen hours," he muttered, shaking his head as he walked. I also noticed in the corner of that emergency room that my mom stirred. I don't think she appreciated his outburst much.

"Young lady, do you know you should have died two days ago in Lake Huron? There's no scientific reason you should be alive! No way you should be breathing and still on this earth."

Well, he may have been gorgeous, but the train obviously didn't go all the way to the end of the track! He just couldn't see what was right in front of him.

Mr. Dreamy just kept going on and on. To be honest, he was starting to get on my last nerve, and the tears started to fall down my face. Out of the corner of my eye, I could see my mother getting up out of her chair. After all I'd been through, I could see the "mama bear" rising up inside my mom. If this doctor didn't stop soon, he was going to get an earful from Edna Steele! And it wasn't going to be good for him! I decided to interrupt his exultations.

"Doc, no offense, but I'm sure glad you're not in charge." I heard the nurses snickering in the background when I said that to "Mr. Dreamy."

Doc looked down at me on the gurney and patted my shoulder and said, "I'm so sorry, Cheryl, I did not mean to upset you." Thankfully, my mom sat back down.

"But you're so young, you don't understand. . . *you're not supposed to be here.*"

He continued, "You just don't understand. You don't know that people just do not survive in forty-nine-degree water. Have you ever studied the Titanic? Do you realize that they were in twenty-nine-degree water and died, while you just survived *fifteen hours* in forty-nine-degree water? You should've died two days ago. Cheryl, you are a miracle! You're going to be in science books . . ."

He looked out the hospital windows, thoughtful for a minute. "I'm an atheist," he said. "Young lady, you have just rocked my foundation. I'm going to have to go home and rethink a few things, because obviously there is someone above who loves you deeply and who just spared your life."

It was like I could see the light bulb turn on for him.

"Doc, do you have a Bible?" I asked.

"I'll have to knock the dust off of it," he chuckled.

"I can assure you there is life after death. Dust it off." I winked at him! "And I hope you will read the book of John. Then, I think you will see why I have such faith."

Right then and there, it all hit me afresh. I really *should* have died, and I really was spared by some miracle. *Thank you, Lord. I'm alive!* I started to realize that in the graciousness and goodness of God, I had been spared to tell the story, and then to *live* the story.

My mom stayed with me at the hospital through the night, right next to my bed, and slept very little on an uncomfortable green cot, checking on me throughout the night. I remember her hand brushing my forehead a couple of times that night. They discharged me the next day. My bruising was terrible—I looked like I'd been beaten up—but the internal damage to my liver didn't require me to stay another night.

I returned to the camp early that afternoon. Everyone at the camp was obviously grief-stricken. I asked Eldon ("Dad Brock" is what we all called him at camp) if I could speak to all the counselors and staff before I left for home. I needed to encourage them to keep on going on and minister to the campers that God would send to Lake Ann Camp that summer, because that is what Dwight, Sally, and Mark would have wanted. Also, I needed to see them and tell them through wet eyes that I did all I could to bring them back with me. I remember being so weak that I had to use a microphone and sit on a barstool chair. The high-energy, athletic wilderness counselor I had been just a few days before was gone for the time being.

We came home to my house in the Melvindale/Allen Park suburbs of Detroit for recovery Sunday evening. As I came through our kitchen door, my dad greeted me with tears streaming down his face, gently embracing me with a bear hug and not letting go for a few minutes. It was so good to see him! I was finally at home and could begin to truly rest. No longer was I submerged in freezing lake water. No longer was I alone on an island, wandering through the woods. No longer was I laying on a gurney in Canada or even in Traverse City. I was home and in my own bed.

But there was so much recovery ahead. And so many unanswered questions. Why had this happened? How could three of my friends be dead? How would the camp recover from such a tragic and searing loss?

I pulled the covers up and fell into a very restless and fitful sleep.

State of Michigan
Department of Social Services
Lansing, Michigan 48926

The provider shall report to the Department of Social Services any serious accident or illness requiring admission to a hospital which occurs while the facility is in operation. In case of a fatality the cause of death must be included in this report.

1. NAME OF FACILITY OR PROVIDER		2. PROVIDER NUMBER
Regular Baptist Camp of Michigan, Inc.		

3. FACILITY ADDRESS (Street, City, Zip)	4. COUNTY	5. PHONE
Lake Ann MI	Benzie	

6. NAME OF INJURED CHILD OR ADULT	7. HOME ADDRESS (Street, City, Zip, Phone)	8. AGE	9. SEX
Cheryl Steele	Melvindale, MI	21	☐ Male ☒ Female

10. NAME OF WITNESS (If more than one, print on back)	11. HOME ADDRESS (Street, City, Zip)	12. PHONE
None except for her		

13. ACCIDENT OR ILLNESS	14. WHERE DID ACCIDENT HAPPEN?
(Date) (Time)	In Sitgreaves Bay or Pilot
Began 7/3/80 3:00 p.m. ended 7/4/80 12:30 p.m.	on the N.E. of Drummond Island

15. DESCRIBE INJURY OR ILLNESS

Exhaustion and internal injuries

16. WHAT CAUSED THE ACCIDENT TO HAPPEN? WHAT WAS THE CHILD/ADULT DOING?

A group of four were crossing the Sitgreaves Bay going east when the winds shifted from behind them to be against them and also increased. This blew them out away from the island. Later they decided to head for Cockburn island. She was found on Cockburn Island by people in a private yacht. She had survived 13 hours in the water and 5 or 6 of looking for help on the shore of Cockburn Island.

17. WHAT FIRST AID WAS GIVEN AND/OR ACTION WAS TAKEN?

After they were blown into rough seas, they used all preventative and surviv. measures.

18. HOW WAS INJURY OR ILLNESS DIAGNOSED BY PHYSICIAN?	20. WERE ANY HANDICAPS, HEALTH PROBLEMS OR EXCEPTIONS LISTED ON CHILD'S/ADULT'S HEALTH RECORDS ☒ NO ☐ YES IF YES, EXPLAIN:
Exhaustion and internal injury to liver.	

19. NAME OF DIAGNOSING PHYSICIAN	
Traverse City, MI	

21. IF FATALITY, CAUSE OF DEATH

22. LOCAL CORONER NOTIFIED	23. AUTOPSY PERFORMED
☐ YES ☐ NO	☐ YES ☐ NO

24. AFTER THINKING ABOUT THE ACCIDENT/ILLNESS, IS THERE ANY ACTION YOU WOULD SUGGEST TO PREVENT IT FROM HAPPENING AGAIN?

Not to allow canoes off shore in these waters. This was a staff exploring party of 4 and had planned before leaving Lake Ann camp to stay on lakes on Drummond Island

25. SIGNATURE OF PERSON COMPLETING REPORT	26. TITLE	27. DATE

28. SIGNATURE OF PROVIDER OR OPERATOR		29. DATE
Eldon Brock, Exec Admin.		7-8-80

A report to the State of Michigan Department of Social Services signed by Eldon Brock. He worked tirelessly on all matters relating to the tragedy on my behalf and on that of the Coons, Taubes, and Herzbergers.

10

GMCs

POWER OF A PRAYING PARENT—DURING THE STORMY NIGHT—EDNA STEELE

Five weeks later, my mom told me a story about the night of July 3, 1980. She was at her home in Melvindale, fast asleep like any other night. For some reason she woke up around quarter to five. In her own words, "I just knew something was wrong with Carolyn."

Carolyn is one of my older sisters. She is hilarious and has such a giving heart! At that time in Carolyn's life, she wasn't making good decisions. She was partying a lot, and Mom believed she was experimenting with drugs. We all love her and prayed for God's direction in her life.

That night, my mom woke up, got a drink of water, and felt the Holy Spirit impress something on her heart: "Go pray for your daughter. You've got to intercede right now. She's in trouble." My mom didn't hear an audible voice, she just knew God was telling her, "go pray for your daughter."

Assuming that Carolyn had gotten herself into a dangerous place, my mom obediently prayed for her daughter. Mom told me that she got down her knees in her living room next to her recliner and started praying: *Oh Lord, please don't take my middle daughter, Carolyn. I know she's in trouble tonight, Lord. She's got a story to tell. Don't take her. Wherever she's at, Lord, let her get home safe. Oh Lord, please don't take my middle daughter, Carolyn. Let her live to live your legacy.*

Little did she know that the one she was praying for was her youngest daughter—me! I was 450 miles away from mom at that time, praying to the same God.

I've heard people challenge the existence of God over the years. But when I think about my mom's story, I have no doubt that God is real. Shortly after my body was finally giving in to hypothermia—the early morning hours of July 4, 1980, the time when I was falling asleep in a stormy, freezing lake, and right around the time when I was faced with one of the toughest decisions of my life (to swim for Cockburn Island)—my mom is inexplicably woken up and overcome with a sensation that God is telling her to pray for her daughter to live and come home.

Now, you tell me there's no God! I believe without a doubt that my mom interceded for me that night. And I'm so grateful. Whenever I tell this story to students or adults, I always say, "If you've got a parent that prays for you, then you go home and kiss them tonight. Tell them you love them. There is power in a praying parent."

My question for you is, have you ever felt God calling you to intercede for someone else? Have you ever felt like God was speaking to your heart like He spoke to my mom's?

You never know what someone might be going through. You just never know what each day has in store, or if God may call on you to stand in the gap for someone in trouble. So don't shake that feeling off and think it is just you. Pray right then and there for the person or situation. You never know . . . and I believe God does answer prayers!

FAITH

You have to have great faith through all the battering storms (wave by wave) and trials during your life. My trials were unique, but yours, the story that God has for you, they are unique too. I truly believe God has a story for each one of us. It's yours to live out and give God the glory for.

HOPE

During that night I never once thought that Dwight and Sally didn't make it. Maybe in my subconscious mind, I wondered if they had gone on to be with the Lord in heaven, but during that night I never let my conscious mind think that they didn't make it. I prayed and prayed, hoping that they had made it to the island or that someone had picked them up. I never gave up hope for a fisherman or that we were somehow going to get help.

I knew Sally wasn't as strong as Dwight. I knew she'd been sunburned the day before and wondered if maybe this had affected how quickly hypothermia set in for her. And I'd heard Dwight's incoherent speech myself.

Yet, I never let myself think that both of them hadn't made it.

GET OUT OF THE CANOE!

We all have tough decisions in our lives, whether young or old. When faced with crossroads in our life, family, with work, health, relationships, parents, children—whatever it be—decisions have to be made.

In my lifetime I have challenged my students, and all age groups that I have spoken to, that we all have our "canoe moments." Mine was literally in a canoe on a stormy night in freezing cold water in Lake Huron. I had to decide to stay with the canoe and hope my situation changed for the better, or to risk it and get out and swim toward better, and for me, literally my life.

If you do not like things the way they are in your life, do not be afraid to "get out of the canoe" of your comfort zone and go for better. I know it will be hard, but change can only come when we decide to move into action. Life is too short to be miserable. I believe in God, and I always pray that He will direct my paths. He gave me legs to walk into a better future.

So what are you waiting for? *Get out* of the *canoe!*

GOD-MADE COINCIDENCES—LIFE IS FULL OF THESE IF WE JUST BE STILL, WATCH AND LISTEN DURING OUR LIVES

There are no coincidences in life—not really. They're all God-made. I call these God-Made Coincidences, or GMCs.

I've learned that you can't go through life so fast that you don't enjoy every moment. And you don't notice what God might be doing in the "coincidences" around you. But things can change so quickly. Life can change on a dime. When we left that week, I had no idea that I'd be the only one to come back.

For example, my mom prayed for me on the very night that my body temperature was so low I was at death's door. She was prompted to pray for me right at the exact time when my body was facing its final test: a mile and a half swim through frigid waters after surviving a ten-hour storm. Was this just a coincidence? No. What I take from this is that when the Holy Spirit taps on your shoulder to pray, then you pray. That's a GMC. The Lord gave my precious mother her peace after her prayer and she went back to bed. She didn't have any earthly idea that by following this prompting from God, she was stepping right into a GMC. And I'm so glad she did!

Was it a random coincidence that the sun was shining brightly on me that morning on Cockburn Island? Just when I needed warmth more than ever? If it would have been rainy or cold that morning, I could have died. My core body temperature was dangerously low when my feet hit Cockburn Island that morning. Right then, I needed an external source to warm me. That was a GMC.

I am truly grateful that God sent the s-u-n to warm my body up that day, but even if He hadn't, I know the S-o-n had already saved me.

I hope you will stop daily, breathe easily, and listen quietly. If you listen for the Holy Spirit's guidance during your life, then you'll find GMCs too.

"And we know that God causes everything to work together for the good of those who love God and are called according to his purpose for them" (Romans 8:28 NLT).

11

WHAT'S THE PURPOSE?

I n the years since the tragedy, I've stayed in contact with Jim
and Donna Coon as well as other members of Sally's family.[7]
I asked Jim to share some of his stories about the events in
this book, including how he and Donna heard the news of Sally's
death:

> July 4, 1980, started out as a fun day. Donna and I drove
> fifty miles to Mackinaw City, Michigan (a well-known
> tourist destination), with two of our eight children, Steve
> and Diane, just for something to do on the holiday.
>
> After spending time in Mackinaw, we decided to
> travel fifteen miles back to Cheboygan, Michigan, where we
> had lived for seven years, and where we had started Faith
> Baptist Church in our living room. We had many friends
> in Cheboygan, including Bill and Carole Lee and their five
> children, plus our pastor, Larry McCaly, and his four children.
>
> Bill and Carole owned markets in several towns
> in Northern Michigan, known as B&C Supermarkets.
> We drove to a B&C parking lot that overlooked the local
> fairgrounds where the fireworks were soon to be. Pastor

McCaly and his wife were leaning on the front of their car. We pulled up alongside them to say hi.

"Bill Lee is looking for you," Pastor said, "and also the state police."

We proceeded to park by the shopping center just as Bill and Carole drove up. Carole got out of the car and took Donna and our two children into the foyer of the market (it was closed). Bill exited his car at the same time as I did. Bill is short with words. It didn't take long before I knew why they were looking for us. Bill put his arm around my shoulder and said, "Sally died."

I have never been able to cry (a man's thing, I guess) but at that moment, tears rushed down my face for just seconds, then it was over.

My heart heard God's voice. It was not audible, but He said, "Jim, I don't make mistakes."

I looked up and repeated it: "God, I know you don't make mistakes."

"If I don't make mistakes," He said, "then what's the purpose?"

Again, I looked up and repeated that question, "What's the purpose?" God spoke to my heart again.

"You and your friends get out of the way, and I'll show you."

This entire message didn't take more than two minutes. I entered the supermarket where Donna was and related what I just experienced. We left soon after to return to Gaylord and to start informing our loved ones. It started to rain and thunder, which prompted our young children to say (after one loud thunderclap), "I think Sally has found a bowling alley!"

They knew their sister loved to bowl. We all knew that Sally was finally at home.

BRING HEALING TO THE HURTING

God continued to speak to Jim and others in the Coon family through His Word, the Bible. Jim shared with me the following passages of Scripture:

Therefore, strengthen your feeble arms and weak knees. "Make level paths for your feet," so that the lame may not be disabled, but rather healed. (Hebrews 12:12–13)

Jim said, "Draw from Christ's strength, then we can use our growing strength to *help those around us* who are weak and struggling." He also shared this verse with me:

> Strengthen the feeble hands,
> steady the knees that give way;
> say to those with fearful hearts:
> "Be strong, do not fear;
> your God will come.
> Isaiah 35:3–4

More from Jim, "In essence, God was saying to me through these verses, 'through Christ, I will give you all the strength you'll need to bring healing to the hurting.'"

I am amazed by this emphasis Jim and Donna placed on other people's needs in the wake of losing one of their precious children. Bring healing to the hurting.

JULY 4, 1980. JACKSON, MICHIGAN.

The following story is from Mark's dad, Dan Taube:

We were living in the New Tribes Bible School building that summer. [Dan was both a contractor who was helping New Tribes Mission renovate different buildings in Jackson for their missionary training programs, as well as a teacher in what they called "Boot Camp" for soon-to-be missionaries.]

There weren't many people who lived in the building like we did. And it was July 4th, a holiday, so there were even fewer people than was typical. I heard someone banging on the main entry door. I was surprised to see Pastor Mike Bracey from Michigan Center Bible Church as well as a pastor from another church in Jackson. Somehow, they had gotten word about the tragedy. They came to tell us.

We were *stunned.* "Your son's body has been found," they said. And Dwight and Sally too. We knew Dwight of course, but we didn't know Sally. . .

It was gut-wrenching. Donna and I were 39 at the time. We knew the Lord had it . . . but it was *not pleasant.*

[As painful as this story is, Dan recounted it with warmth in his voice.]

It seemed like a good thing to send our son to camp, and then . . . he's not coming back. At first, we were thinking, *well, as parents it's our job to keep our kids from getting into serious or bad situations.* So, we felt responsible for a while. But really. . . the Lord knows.

SUSTAINING FAITH

Both Dwight's parents, Bud and Bertie Herzberger, have since passed away and went on to be with the Lord. But shortly after the accident, I went to their home, stayed the night, and talked with them. They were such sweet people. I can still remember Bertie's eyes as we talked until early morning in her living room about Dwight. (Her husband, Bud, had since gone to bed.) I remember the twinkle in her beautiful eyes, and I knew where Dwight got his eyes and terrific sense of humor!

The hardest thing I have ever done is sit across from three sets of parents who wanted to know the last detailed moments of their child's lives on this earth. I could see the grief in their eyes and hear it in their voices as we spoke.

As a mother myself now, to two awesome young men (Robbie and Jeff), I can't imagine what this was like for the Coons, Herzbergers, and Taubes. No parent wants to go after their children. The way it should go is that our children eventually bury us, and our children and their children live on. These three sets of parents, siblings, and their families were and still are amazing people with great faith in our Heavenly Father. They have had many hard days, and yet their faith sustained them through those hard days and still does. I know what you are thinking— *there must be something to a God who "heals the brokenhearted."*

TRUE TO HIS WORD

J im Coon didn't know what to expect when he heard God say to his heart, "You and your friends get out of the way, and I'll show you." Well, God was true to His word and surpassed everyone's expectations.

God's work began at Dwight, Sally, and Mark's funerals. I didn't get to attend any of the three funerals. They were all held shortly after the accident in their respective hometowns. I was still in terrible shape, injured and recuperating. As much as it would have meant to go to all three funerals, I had to stay home and build back my strength. So, the stories I'm going to relate here were told to me after the fact. Each one speaks of God's power to bring good things out of a tragic situation.

TO DIE IS GAIN

Sally's funeral was unique for a couple of reasons. The first was that those in attendance were able to listen to Sally share what Christians call her *testimony*—the story of when and why she placed her faith in Jesus Christ as the Son of God, and as her personal Savior from sin. Her testimony had been recorded at

Lake Ann, just a few weeks prior to the accident. All of those mourning her loss were able to hear, in her own words, about her faith in God. A brief moment of levity came when she said on the recording that, while she was raised in a Christian home, she didn't want to accept Christ yet because she wanted to wait until she "had a really good testimony."

Another reason this funeral was unique came in the form of a short story. A close friend of the Coon family is a man named Kenneth Bradstreet. Ken is a writer, and he was deeply moved by the loss of Sally. Like the Coons themselves, Ken's faith assured him of exactly where Sally was at that moment—she was in the presence of her Savior, Jesus. So, he wrote a story that envisioned Sally's first conversations with her Lord and gave it to Jim and Donna. They were so moved by the story that they printed it and handed it out in a small pamphlet at her funeral and visitation.

~~~~~

"Sally . . . Sally, do you hear me?"

"Yes. Who are you?"

"I've been sent to show you home. I have been sort of looking after you these past few years—since you trusted Jesus as Savior. Just this morning He told me you would be coming home."

"I guess I don't quite understand. But it sure is good to be rescued. That was quite an ordeal! Are the others all safe?"

"Yes, they're all safe. In fact, two of them will be coming home with us."

"Home? To Gaylord?"

"No, Sally, not Gaylord. Home for the child of God is Heaven—where Jesus is. We must go now. He's very anxious to talk to you. In fact, He is just up ahead and waiting for you."

"I think I understand now what's happening. But I'm afraid to meet Jesus. What do I say to Him? My sin . . . I don't think I'm really ready for this."

"Sally, it's normal for you to feel that way. Everyone does. But remember, Sally, as far as Jesus is concerned, you are ready. In fact, you are perfect—without sin. Remember His promise which you claimed, that He would forgive all your sins and not just forgive—He has promised to forget them as well. He no longer even knows about your sin. He has taken it all away. Your fellowship with Him can be complete and perfect now. Anyway, your fears are temporary. As soon as you see Him face to face your fears will be gone. His love is so perfect—it casts out all fear. Look, Sally. Here He is now. . . . Lord, Sally is here as you have requested."

"Sally! I've looked forward to this time ever since we first met. We have so much to talk about. But first I want to show you your new home which I have been getting ready for you. I think you will like it. It's right this way. You can see it now as we get closer."

"Jesus, this is beautiful. I could never have imagined anything like it. Jesus, you know I was afraid to meet you at first, but I have never experienced happiness like this before. Jesus, do you really have time to talk just to me? I want so to get to know you better."

"Yes, Sally. I have all the time you desire. You know, this is why I made you in the first place. From this time on our fellowship will be complete. There is no sin here to come between us . . .

"Sally, are you interested in taking a short trip with me? There are services in your honor and I've been invited to attend. Actually, I am there already, but I don't expect you to comprehend that. I would like to have you join me if you care to."

"I don't know if I want to or not. I can't bear to see the sorrow. My family and friends don't all understand about Heaven–what a beautiful and happy place this is, with your love and all."

"I am with them right now too, don't forget. And I would like you to see how great the peace that passes all understanding works. Will you come with me?"

"I'll go anywhere you want. I don't ever want to leave you."

"Sally, you need not worry about that. There will never be an end to our fellowship and love. That's what eternal life is all about. Come, now. We'll be there in just a very short time."

"Jesus, I never expected this many people. Are they all here for me?"

"Yes, Sally. You know, you are very special. . . . Let me explain something. This is how I work many times. As you know, people are very different from the way you are now. Their memories are quite short and they get sidetracked easily. Often they get to thinking only in terms of this earthly life and they seem to get caught up with this world. When this happens, I have to remind them of Heaven. Quite often I will take someone home who is really extra special to them and to me. Only then, when I have their attention, can I speak to them. In fact, I have already been able to speak to many of them and remind them about me and eternal life. All of these people here are today reminded of me and of Heaven—and all because of you. Remember your favorite portion from my Word? 'Christ shall be magnified in my body, whether it be by life, or by death.' Through your death, I am being glorified in a great way. And I have only started to work.

"Sally, I think we should go home now. I want to talk to you some more. I have so much to tell you of the many great things that I will be doing very soon as a result of your life—in Gaylord, among your friends and family and at Lake Ann. Because of you I'll be able to get the attention of so many people. Then I can speak to them of things which are truly important. Many of them do not know me and some of them who have met me do not really know me very well. I will be talking to many of them while they are listening."

"Jesus, I know you know best, and I can't wait to hear what you are going to do. I'm ready to go back home."

Philippians 1:20–23, KJV:

> According to my earnest expectation and my hope, that in nothing I shall be ashamed, but that with all boldness, as always, so now also Christ shall be magnified in my body, whether it be by life, or by death. For to me to live is Christ, and to die is gain. But if I live in the flesh, this is the fruit of my labour, yet what I shall choose I wot not. For I am in a strait betwixt two, having a desire to depart, and to be with Christ; which is far better.[8]

The response to Sally's testimony and Ken's story was *incredible*. Right there at the casket side, people started getting *saved*! People who had never called themselves a Christian confessed their sins to God, placed their trust in Jesus's sacrifice for their salvation, and dedicated their lives to following Jesus from that point on.

Souls were not the only thing saved at the funeral that day. Marriages were too! Right at the funeral, couples who were going to separate decided to reconcile. Just like at the camp, everyone at the funeral seemed to ask themselves the same question, What would I leave behind if I were to die today?

A local newspaper, *The Herald Times,* reported on the events of the funeral:

> The strength displayed by Jim and Donna Coon and their children is no personal characteristic, but rather is because of their faith in God. "In Feb. of 1978, Sally committed her life and gave her life to God by accepting Christ as her personal Savior," her father said. In doing that, she was prepared for Heaven.[9]

Sally's loss was *profound.* There is no doubt that the grief Jim and Donna, her seven siblings, and the whole community experienced was intense. But God *immediately* began to use the loss of her life to spread grace and hope. God demonstrated to Jim, to me, and to everyone else who has heard about Sally's life that He keeps His promises.

One of Sally's sisters, Carole Ulrich, said of the funeral: "The way our family handled it . . . there was such a peace there. It was an honor to have the Lord present at the funeral. You could feel it. Yeah, there were tears, but there was joy too. And there were great stories."

Sally's favorite Bible passage is the one listed above, Philippians 1:20–23. After her death the Coons found several quotes that had been penned in the margin of her Bible and dated just two weeks before her death. Next to these verses in Philippians, Sally had written:

"Christ has a purpose for us here on earth and He won't take us home until it is accomplished."

"What has happened to me will become my deliverance."

*A picture of Sally given to me by her parents, Jim and Donna
Coon.*

HOMEGOING

If you're already a believer in Jesus, then you've likely heard of
heaven described as "home." This idea comes from numerous
passages in the Bible. Perhaps some of the most well-known are
Philippians 3:20, which says, "our citizenship is in heaven," as
well as John 14:1–3, in which Jesus says:

Do not let your hearts be troubled. You believe in God; believe also in me. My Father's house has many rooms; if that were not so, would I have told you that I am going there to prepare a place for you? And if I go and prepare a place for you, I will come back and take you to be with me that you also may be where I am.

So, when a believer like my friend Sally dies, it's not uncommon for us to think of death as a homegoing. Death for the believer isn't blinking out of existence. It's not a slow decay into nothingness. While our body might turn to dust, for our soul it is the first step into eternal life with God in our true home. Death is a homegoing!

But that doesn't mean it's easy for those of us left behind after loved ones go home, especially if the manner of someone's death was tragic. Since that terrible night in 1980, many people have asked the question that Jim Coon mentioned in his story: What's the purpose of this tragedy? Did Dwight, Sally, and Mark really have to die? For what reasons would God need to bring three young Christians to their home in heaven?

I'd like to share a few more stories from Jim Coon which might point us toward an answer.

John and Phyllis Cheny lived in the small farming community of Elmira, Michigan. John was the postmaster. The Chenys had one child, Marcy, who married a rugged, hardworking man named David Gorney. Together, they had five children. All of them were members of St. Frances Catholic Church, the only church in town.

At some point, John and Phyllis invited Christ into their lives. After that, their focus turned to their only child and her family. They began to, in Marcy's terms, "badger" her to the point that Marcy put her foot down.

"If you talk to me anymore about 'religion,'" she said, "I will stop coming over." They lived less than a football field from each other. This would mean not having contact with the grandchildren. This was of great concern to John and Phyllis.

The Chenys also began looking for a new church, where they would feel more "fed" by the Scriptures, and where they could use their talents in service for God. Eventually they settled on Calvary Baptist Church in Gaylord, eleven miles to the east of Elmira.

On Wednesdays at Calvary Baptist the Chenys would attend a short teaching from the Bible, followed by small groups separating for prayer. Sally's mother, Donna, along with Phyllis Cheny and another woman named Darlene Jones formed a small group for prayer. Among the things they prayed about was that Phyllis's daughter, Marcy, would come invite Christ into her life, just as John and Phyllis had. Donna prayed urgently for Marcy, saying, "whatever it takes, we want to see Marcy get saved." This was on Wednesday, July 2, 1980.

After Sally's homegoing on July 3, 1980, we held a customary showing of Sally's body on July 7, from 6:00 p.m. to 9:00 p.m. We were so overwhelmed with folks coming and not wanting to leave that the funeral director stayed open an extra hour. Dave and Marcy Gorney came like most people (it's the right thing to do in a small town). At this point, many people were caught up asking the question, "What's the purpose?"

Dave and Marcy must have been asking that question too. They left the showing eager to attend the funeral service the next day, July 8, 1980. Early that morning, Marcy called her mom to see if they could talk with the pastor.

Marcy fulfilled Donna's urgent request and relieved John and Phyllis's burden—she invited Christ into her life. One month later, Dave was at a playground park, sitting on a picnic table alone and also asked Jesus into his life. Several months after that, Dave sold his business and moved the family to Wisconsin where he enrolled in a Bible College."

Sally's body was laid to rest at Pine View Cemetery in Gaylord, Michigan. Her headstone reads, "To God be the glory." The homegoing of someone so young begs the question, What's the purpose? I think God has been showing us all the answer for many years!

THE GREATEST USE
OF LIFE

I do not know if it was the US Coast Guard, someone from the police station in Drummond, or someone from Canada, but my backpack was eventually found floating in Lake Huron. It was shipped back to Lake Ann Camp. Eldon Brock (along with my good friend Jeff Tindall) came to visit at my family home in the Downriver, Detroit area and gave it back to me. I was *thrilled* to discover that my camera was not harmed. I developed the film a few weeks later and found the picture of Dwight and Mark that I'd taken on the Monday in camp before we headed to Drummond that July 4 week (see photo on page 27). Mark has his arm slung over his mentor and friend, wearing a confident half-smile and a cowboy hat. Dwight's smiling too, behind his aviator sunglasses. It's tragic to think that was the last picture taken of either of them. Yet, I'm thankful to God that we have the picture at all. The fact that we could even *find* my backpack, or that the camera was unharmed, is a miracle in and of itself.

DWIGHT'S PASSION FOR CAMPERS

Ken Riley has worked at Lake Ann Camp for more than thirty years and has served as the executive director since 1992. (He, his wife Margy, and his family have been good friends to me and my family all these years. He is an outstanding leader for the camp!) But before he became the executive director, he and Dwight were counselors together at Lake Ann in 1978, the year before I joined the staff. Ken and Dwight became good friends and stayed close, even after Ken took a job in 1979 as a youth pastor at a church in Iowa. Ever the writer, Dwight kept up the friendship by writing long, often humorous letters to Ken.

"I can still remember one of his letters," Ken said. "He began with, 'I'm writing this from the hospital. I got my students during lunch hour to take their lunch trays and went to a hill [to slide in the snow]. Now, you rarely made it to the bottom [on a lunch tray] but I'd finally made it to the bottom once, just in time to hear "look out!" and I got run over by a toboggan with six people on it. So, I'm in the hospital right now . . .' Now that's something that *only* Dwight could write. Something like that would only happen to *Dwight*."

"Lots of times people only saw his funny, goofy side," Ken continued. "But underneath all that was a guy who loved the Lord and really wanted to make Christ known."

Dwight is remembered not only as someone who believed in God but as someone who truly believed in the camp experience for teens. Here's another story from Ken Riley that demonstrates Dwight's care for others:

> During the summer of 1978, while Dwight and I were both on staff, there was this one counselor that thought he was more spiritual than everybody else. He'd been studying

foolishness in the book of Proverbs and as a result, he would not participate in the skit nights. He thought the skit nights were "foolishness."

Camp counselors often performed skits for campers as a way to make them laugh while imparting spiritual truths. They may be funny, even goofy, but the goal is to impart wisdom, not foolishness.

Dwight was concerned about the perception the campers were going to have because of this counselor's attitude. So, Dwight went to the camp director and sought permission for he and I to speak, respectfully, to this counselor about the effect his choice was having on the campers. Dwight talked the director into it, and we went and had the conversation. It's an example of Dwight's love for the campers and his belief that God could do something amazing in the lives of a student while they were at camp.

Some people would only see his goofy side. But he cared so much about the campers, and their experience, that he was not afraid of confrontation if it was necessary.

One of Dwight's favorite verses was Galatians 6:14:

As for me, may I never boast about anything except the cross of our Lord Jesus Christ. Because of that cross, my interest in this world has been crucified, and the world's interest in me has also died. (NLT)

Dwight also wrote the following in one of his journals. He was an avid reader and loved philosopher/educators like William James. So he used one of his mottoes, and it was his life motto: "The greatest use of life is to spend it for something that will outlast it."

Dwight Herzberger

GRIEF FOR THE TAUBES

Dan Taube recounted a meeting I had with he and his wife Donna in 1980: "A couple months after Mark's death we went over to Cheryl's house and spent a Sunday afternoon with her. She gave us the blow-by-blow description [of the tragedy] . . . The fact that she managed to survive the water and get to the island is amazing. If Cheryl had died too, I always would've been asking, 'how did this happen?'"

Friends from New Tribes Missions and their local church donated money to the Taubes to help cover funeral costs. As well as the cost of flying Mark's body back to Iowa for a funeral at the Taube's home church (one of the places they lived before they moved to Jackson, Michigan) and burial next to his maternal grandmother in the family plot.

"There were three funerals for Mark," Dan Taube said. "We went out to the camp for a service. Dwight's parents (Bertie and Bud Herzberger) and Sally's parents (Jim and Donna Coon) were there too. Some of Mark's shoes were there. It was a grief to us [to see his shoes]. It was the first thing we'd seen of Mark's clothes.

"Once his body got back to Jackson, we had a funeral at Michigan Center Bible Church. Then we drove his body out to Iowa and we had a funeral there. It was hard, but it seemed like the thing to do. The first few months it just takes a while before you can really find humor in anything. Everything becomes a little more grim, but in time it becomes okay."

WHO WILL FILL THESE SHOES?

The memorial service Dan Taube described was held in Traverse City. Trudy Brock (Eldon's wife—we all called her "mom") laid out three pairs of shoes in front of the pulpit. One pair was

Dwight's. One pair was Sally's. One pair was Mark's. With these physical reminders of the loss in front of the staff, Eldon Brock shared a powerful message to "fill these shoes." He challenged the staff to "live filling these shoes."

What a powerful, emotional reminder of not only the loss we all experienced, but of our new responsibility to step in where Dwight, Sally, and Mark would have stood. Despite this tragic and traumatic loss of three staff members, there was still God's work to do at Lake Ann Camp. Campers were still coming—campers who needed to know that God loved them and that Jesus paid the cost of their sins—and Eldon (Dad) Brock asked the staff to step up for God's glory.

Everyone at the camp did. One of the effects of this accident is that everyone seriously considered and reconsidered not only our own relationship with God but the very work we were doing at the camp. My good friend and mentor, Professor Ray (Gator) Gates from GRBC, ran the Teepee Village program at Lake Ann Camp at the time. In his words, "Everyone got more serious about the work."

Sally's father, Jim Coon, told me about an important, specific story connected to this memorial service.

"Director Dad Brock and his wife always interviewed each student counselor to determine their level of spiritual maturity. They became most concerned about a young girl [who was working for the camp].

"As the memorial service concluded, the question was asked, 'who would fill the shoes of those who we are honoring?' They didn't plan that anyone would *literally* fill the shoes. However, this same girl was the only one that asked to try to fill Sally's shoes [and asked if she could keep them]. As time went by, she matured in the Lord. That young lady grew up, got married, and now serves with her husband as missionaries in Central African Republic, John and Paula Dannenberg."

This story makes me think of God's question to Jim the day he heard Sally was gone, What's the purpose?

THE BEST DECISIONS IN LIFE

Here's another story from Sally's dad, Jim Coon, about what God has done in the wake of this tragedy.

A couple named Steve and Joan Swan fit into this story in a unique way. Donna and I became Amway Distributors under the Swan's organization. As a result, we've been friends for life. Shortly after that Sally became involved. Before her death Sally was listing her best decisions up to that point in her life and penned this response: "The two best decisions in my life are inviting Jesus into my life and joining an Amway Family."

As a self-taught pianist, Sally began teaching the Swan's eight-year-old daughter Stacy to play.

Fast forward now to Sally's homegoing. The Swans came to the funeral home alone. Donna and I inquired about their children and encouraged them to bring them back. They went home and did just that, returning with Stacy (eight) and Chris (four).

Fast forward once more to the Memorial Service in Traverse City. The Swans offered to take Donna and I in their motor home so we could talk, and talk we did. After the service and a brief time of fellowship at Lake Ann Camp, we started the hundred-mile trip home.

Donna had Sally's well-used Bible in her hands while seated next to Joan. They never stopped talking. Joan asked many questions, which Donna met with answers from Sally's Bible.

In the meantime, I held Steve's feet to the fire. (He was driving and couldn't get away. Ha!) Both of the Swans invited Jesus into their lives and turned their family in a new direction.

Stacy is now grown and married and has two children. She has been in full-time Christian work since college. Chris majored in music and now ministers in church music and teaches piano, voice, and other instruments.

NIGHTMARES AND MEDIA SHARKS

For the first several weeks after the accident, while I was at home recovering from my injuries, I was haunted by terrible nightmares. They were so intense that I often woke up numerous times in tears and never made it through a night's sleep. Though my body was in desperate need of recovery, my subconscious mind wouldn't let me rest. This went on each night for several weeks that summer. I didn't know if it was ever going to end!

After hearing my story, many people have asked me over the years, "Cheryl, how did you deal with this trauma?"

But I remember one specific Thursday night. I woke up from thrashing and crying and dreaming that I was still in the water. In my dreams I would be reaching for Dwight, Sally, or Mark in the water but could not grab them. I looked at the clock by the nightstand. I remember it was two o'clock. I sat up in my bed, looked up to the ceiling of the bedroom and cried out.

Lord, I have had it! Why in the world did you not let me die in Lake Huron? I cannot take this anymore Lord.

I believe you are God and I know nothing *is impossible with you! I* need, *Lord, for you to take these dreams away! I* cannot *live the rest of my life with this fear of going to sleep only to wake up to nightmares!*

Please, God. please, *Take them away and give me peace,* your peace *about all of this. I put it in your hands and ask that you use everything about the accident to your glory.*

I can tell you that right there in my bedroom, an immense, flowing peace came over my spirit that was supernatural. I did not see anything, but I felt it, the Comforter, the Holy Spirit.

I knew God had answered my prayer. To this day, four decades later, I can emphatically say that I have never had another dream or nightmare about the accident. God took them away right there that Thursday early morning when I was desperate at my lowest point. He is the God of the impossible! And I praise Him!

NEWSPAPER STORIES AND MEDIA SHARKS

A surprising series of events happened when I returned home from Lake Ann. People from all over the US country started calling. Reporters, reporters, reporters. It seemed like everyone wanted to talk to me about what happened. We were getting calls at my parents' house from newspapers across the country as well as radio stations across the world.

Thankfully, my mom and dad put the brakes on all of it. It would have been overwhelming for me if they hadn't. Mom and Dad knew that I needed rest, and I certainly hadn't expected to become a national news story.

My father had always been a fan of the *Detroit Free Press* (never *The Detroit News*). He knew people that worked for the *Free Press*. My brothers had even been newspaper delivery boys.

So, when the reporter from the *Free Press* called and asked, "Do you want to release the story?" I said it would be fine and answered his questions. I didn't know it then, but I would end up on the front page of the *Detroit Free Press* just days after the accident. At that time, the *Free Press* had over a half million circulation each day.

We decided to take only a few interview requests, including one with the *Grand Rapids Press* since I was a student at GRBC and the college's combined teaching curriculum with Calvin College. (Both universities are outstanding!) The *Associated Press* also wrote a story that other papers picked up from the newswire. And I don't know how in the world they did it, but the *Grand Rapids Press* ended up printing a picture of me from high school. "Glad I had a good hair day in high school that day of pictures!" Because my picture was seen in the feature story of over 125,000 papers that day.

Do you know how crazy and unreal it felt to me the weeks after our canoeing accident? The phone was ringing off the hook at my house. My family was answering the phone calls. There were requests for interviews—on air, TV stations from all over, radio stations, and in print—constantly coming in. (This was before the time of individual cell phones, we had just a landline.)

There I was, a twenty-year-old college student working for the summer at a beautiful Christian camp in Northern Michigan, trying to get a grip on what just happened to me, and still recovering, physically and mentally. You open up the daily *Detroit Free Press*—a newspaper that has been delivered to our house every day of my life—and look at the front page of it and see a picture of yourself, a detailed map about what happened, Lake Huron, Drummond Island, the miracle survival and rescue

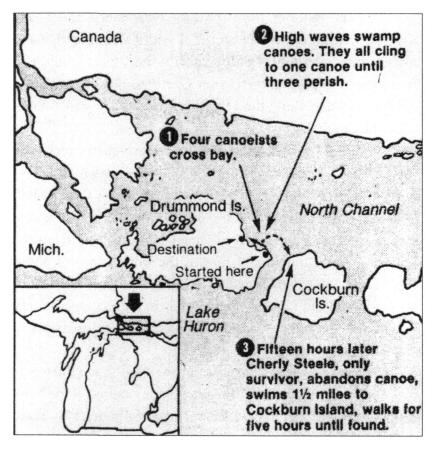

A map describing the accident that ran in the Detroit Free Press.

of this young woman from the suburbs of Detroit. It was mind-blowing to say the least! Even *USA Today*, a national newspaper, included a short story about the accident in one issue.

But to most interview requests we said, "no thank you," and just tried to focus on recovery and rest. There was one reporter from a newspaper who was especially dogged. She was from a paper I'd never heard of before called the *National Enquirer*.

Now remember, it was 1980 and I was just twenty years old. A Christian kid from a small town. I'd never read the *National Enquirer*. I knew nothing about them! I had *no idea* that it was a tabloid paper, known for publishing sensational or fictional stories. I thought it was just another newspaper.

A woman from the *Enquirer* actually came out to the house and she was a *shark*. Talk about pushy people! After I realized what the *Enquirer* was and what she wanted to do with the story I said, "Absolutely not. No, I will not release this. I'm sorry, I'm not into sensationalism. I have nothing against you, but I had no idea what the paper you work for is all about."

The reporter stayed for just a few minutes. I remember her standing on the porch and she said, "I just want to tell you something, Cheryl, I can write this with your permission *or without it*."

"Look, I'm going to tell you something," I said. "I believe God took my friends home."

I tried to talk and witness to her as best I could. I ended with saying, "Ma'am, you have to live with your conscience because I don't want any part of this." And I just left it at that.

In September that year, I was back at college and my mom called me.

"Cheryl, one of your friends from high school who goes to the University of the Cumberlands in Kentucky just called and wondered how you are doing. I told her you are fine, all things considered."

"Mom, I am just about to head to Kroger's," the local grocery store, "to pick up a few things . . ."

"Honey, I'm so sorry, but I don't think they listened to you." My mom continued, "The *National Enquirer* ran a story. I want you to know that you might encounter that." Evidently my friend had seen it and called my mom. Well, I didn't think anything of it. I thought, *Nah, that lady couldn't have done that*, and headed out to the store.

Guess what I saw in Kroger's?

Right at the checkout lanes, smack dab in front of me. Sure enough, there was a blurb on the front page of the *Enquirer* and a full story on the third and fourth pages. I was horrified by what I found. Someone had *staged photographs* for a sensationalized story of the accident. One picture I remember was in reference to "her dead friend's boots." It was an image of a pair boots on a body, covered up and out at a lake, being taken from a gurney. *Unreal.*

"What a bunch of crap!" I stifled my tears until I got in my car in the parking lot. I could not believe it!

But here was the really bad part. I had to call each of the parents—the Herzbergers, the Taubes, and the Coons—and let them know that I did *not* give the *Enquirer* any authority to print that story. I told them all that I was so sorry this happened, that I received no money for it, and that all of it was *crap*. It was heartbreaking and humiliating. All of us were still in the early days of grief. This decision by the *National Enquirer* only added to our pain. I was so angry about the whole thing. They had taken advantage of me and were trying to make money off of the deaths of Dwight, Mark, and Sally. It was the seediest thing I'd ever seen.

My parents called our lawyer, Martin, a family friend from the Detroit area. We wanted to find out what we could do. Were there any legal steps we could take against the *Enquirer*? Should we sue them? This is liable, right? Surely there was something we could do.

Our lawyer came back to us with grim news. He said to my mom, "Edna, they've got probably forty lawyers on staff because they write stories like these. You don't have enough money for your daughter to fight back." To take legal action against an entity like the *National Enquirer* was simply out of reach for our family.

"Just tell Cheryl, I am so sorry, she has to go through this ——, —— (he used a lot of expletives). We can't fight them. You do not have enough money. That is why they do what they do!"

I remember crying on the phone as I spoke with Dwight, Mark, and Sally's parents. I was so afraid of what they might

God has a lot to say about truth and lies in the Bible. You're probably aware that "do not tell lies" is one of the Ten Commandments.[10] But God doesn't just want *us* to live truthfully, God wants us to know that truthfulness is one of His attributes—part of His very nature.

Jesus called himself "the way and the truth and the life."[11] While the book of Hebrews reminds us "it is impossible for God to lie."[12] Meanwhile, the devil is called "the father of lies."[13]

My point? Being a follower of Jesus is a life spent striving after the truth and lifting up the truth. In what parts of your life are you living untruthfully? I really have to examine myself many times, and ask myself: "Cheryl, are your motives 'pure' and 'true?'"

We are all human and we are all sinners. And let's be honest with ourselves and the Lord. Ask God for His help to live in truth, and pray. I promise, He is never too busy to hear you.

think of me, and so upset and angry to think about how this tabloid paper was going to add to their pain.

"It's okay, Cheryl," each of them told me in their own ways. "They took advantage of you."

To my knowledge, none of the families ever read the *Enquirer* story. It just hurt so much to feel taken advantage of in that way. Everything they printed was sensational and done to fit their narrative just to sell more papers. It was fake journalism before the fake journalism we know today.

Camp recovers from shock of deaths

By BILL McCULLOCH
Record-Eagle staff writer

LAKE ANN — Normal summer activity has resumed at the Regular Baptist Youth Camp in northern Benzie County despite the shock brought on by a Lake Huron canoeing accident that took the lives of three camp staff members late last week.

The 210 junior high school-age youngsters attending the current camp session were out in the sunshine Wednesday afternoon, noisily engaged in games of soccer, softball and volleyball — a marked contrast to the mood that prevailed three days earlier when campers were told about the deaths.

News of the tragedy was first relayed to camp personnel by Canadian police last Fri-

day evening, according to John Bush, a maintenance supervisor who was helping to run the camp early this week while director Eldon Brock attended funeral services for the three accident victims.

"The director called me to his house late Friday, told me to sit down, and then said that three of our people had drowned," Bush reported Tuesday. "It was quite a shock. I didn't sleep any that night and I'm sure the director didn't either."

The three victims, who actually died of exposure and hypothermia after their canoes were swamped in False Detour Channel near Drummond Island, were identified as Dwight Herzberger, 27, of Bay City, Sally Coon, 22, of Gaylord, and Mark Taube, 17, of Jackson.

A fourth member of the group, 20-year-old

Cheryl Steele of downstate Melvindale, survived the Thursday accident and is resting at her suburban Detroit home. Bush said the young woman is planning to rejoin the camp staff in about 10 days, when she'll take a group of senior campers on a trip down the Pine River.

Steele and her three dead companions were all working in the Regular Baptist Camp's wilderness program. They had gone to the Drummond Island area in hopes of finding an easier access route to a wilderness campsite on the east end of the island. Bush said a group of campers had packed in to the campsite about a week earlier, but no campers were involved in last Thursday's accident.

(Please turn to Page 3)

Steele

Image from a story that ran in the Traverse City Record-Eagle not long after the accident.

IMPACT IN
GRAND RAPIDS

Sally attended Grand Rapids Baptist College for just one semester before the summer of 1980. During those months she would have her daily quiet time with God in a unique spot. As Jim Coon related the story to me:

> Sally and Carol VanTuinen were roommates at the college, and good friends. Sally was very excited about learning as much as she could about the Bible. Carol was a great encourager. It was working well, until Sally would get distracted by other students. She was looking for a quiet place when she checked the boiler room door and found it unlocked. That boiler room became her quiet place for reading the Bible and prayer, until someone else had the same idea. This didn't set well with Sally, and she complained to Carol. Carol responded with a tongue-in-cheek remark, partly in jest: "Just put your name on the door."

Sally did just that. The sign read, "This room is reserved for Sally Coon from 8:00 until—."

121

After her death, the college placed a plaque over the boiler room door in Sally's honor.

This plaque is a small, physical reminder that God is with us everywhere—during our busiest moments, when life is harried and moving at too fast of a pace. Whether we're in the middle of a freezing lake, or quietly shut away in a boiler room for privacy. God is with us.

BACK ON CAMPUS

By the time I returned to GRBC for the fall semester, I had been on the front page of the *Grand Rapids Press* and numerous other newspapers. Not only that, but stories in Christian circles tend to travel fast. There were numerous ties between GRBC and the camp. My survival story was circulating, and the tragic loss of Sally Coon was known among many of the faculty, staff, and students.

I lived in the apartments on the northwest side of a pond that, at that time, sat in the middle of campus. I roomed with Julie Webster Gardinour and Gayle Yarick. God knew who needed to be my roommates! I told Gayle and Julie about the accident and how "crazy" their roommate was going to be this school year adjusting to everything. If they wanted to move out, I totally understood. The lease was in my name.

Julie said, "Cheryl, we love crazy, and adventure, so no worries!"

I had worked with Gayle Yarick at Lake Ann Camp in 1979. She was our horse wrangler. The campers loved Gayle and her gentle spirit. Meanwhile, Julie has been the "Energizer Bunny" since I have known her. (That girl could run like the wind!) I played intercollegiate basketball with Julie at GRBC for three years. We continued to room together until I graduated college.

Today Gayle and Julie are still my besties. I love these two ladies, and I'm so grateful for their friendship for over 40 years!

Also, as you might expect, *everyone* wanted to hear the story. Retelling and retelling it was wearing me down. No one was trying to wear me out, but the emotional toll of reliving the accident with each telling of the story was starting to become more than I could bear.

I contacted Dr. Welch, the school's president, who was someone I admired. His secretary made a time for me to come see him.

"Cheryl, it's so good to see you," he said with a hug. "I was going to call you. I was letting you settle in this school year. I want you to know we've been praying for you." After a few more minutes of catching up, Dr. Welch surprised me with a request. "Would you speak in chapel?"

Oh, Lord Jesus, I immediately prayed nervously. I wasn't sure I could do that. But it didn't take me more than a few minutes in his office before I realized I *had* to do it. I just knew I had to. I had to tell everyone the story at one time. I was so worn out. I felt like a piece of porcelain china about to shatter.

At that time, student chapel services were held in the gymnasium.[14] In addition to the undergraduate students, faculty, and staff from the college, graduate students, faculty, and staff from Grand Rapids Baptist Seminary were also invited. The seminary boasted a couple hundred students at that time. Its building was just across the pond from the undergraduate campus, close to my apartment. All told, I think I spoke to about seven hundred people that day. Talk about nerve-racking! I was scared to death. I was wearing a skirt that day and I remember thinking, *Oh, there's a breeze in here,* as my skirt brushed my legs. Then I realized it wasn't a breeze. I was so nervous I was shaking!

As I remember it, my mentor "Gator" (Prof. Ray Gates) was in the front row, his funny, goofy self smiling at me. He had been my college basketball coach and fellow staffer at Lake Ann Camp. He was there to show his support.

I wasn't the only speaker scheduled for that day. I don't remember who the other speaker was, but he was supposed to be giving the main message for the day.

"Just share for 15 minutes," Dr. Welch said to me. I remember thinking, *My God, that's a long time.*

Dr. Welch must've seen the trepidation on my face because he said, "Cheryl, you are one of our students. So, say what you want to say. This is a life lesson. You tell the story as God wants you to tell it and we'll be back here praying. I know you can do it."

Before I took the stage, I went into a nearby office of one of the coaches for prayer with Dr. Welch and a few other faculty members. They prayed over me, and together we walked into the gym. I was as ready as I ever would be to give my testimony to my fellow GRBC students.

Well, anyone who grew up in church can tell you that sometimes when people share their testimonies, it takes five minutes, and sometimes, it takes a full hour. I don't know how long I spoke that day, but it was longer than Dr. Welch anticipated, and certainly longer than I believed I was capable of. I had been so nervous before getting up behind the microphone. But once I was there, I started speaking and it was like the Holy Spirit just took over. I wasn't as nervous anymore and I just told the story. I tried to hold back my emotions that I knew were about to surface.

I continued with, "I want to tell you that I am not untouchable." I tried to continue speaking, "You know, I didn't . . ." but just then I got choked up. I turned around for a minute and started to cry. Dr. Welch gave me his big smile. I saw that there were three people on the podium praying.

I turned back around, relaxed, told a joke, and everyone laughed. Then I said, "I know some of you are playing the game. You better quit. I never dreamed that I wouldn't have three people with me this fall."

To drive it home, I reminded them of Sally. "My friend and yours was a student here at the college last school year. Now she is gone from this earth! This could happen to anyone."

Sally had gotten her life together the year before she went to camp. The boiler room was where she found a place to be alone with God. That was kind of like her "war room," the place where she not only drew near to God but did the spiritual battles required to leave sin behind and follow Jesus.

We can't know what would've happened if Dwight, Sally, and Mark had lived. Who they would've become, or what they would have done with their lives. However, I've often wondered if Sally would've maybe been a missionary or a very successful Christian businesswoman. She would have served the Lord, I know that!

God took over while I spoke. I was peer to peer and spoke confidently. "Don't play around. If you do not know the Lord as your Savior, you better not leave today before you do. I didn't know I was going to come back to camp without three of my friends, one being our former classmate Sally Coon. We are young, now in college, and always think we will die when we are old. But to all of us seated in this chapel today, I can tell you from experience, you do not have to be old. Death can happen at any time."

"Please know that I'm approachable," I said that day. "I just wanted to tell everyone this story because it's hard to tell people one-on-one every day."

I said thank you for letting me talk today and that I loved them and sat down. Then I learned that I'd spoken for thirty-five minutes! I had no idea so much time had passed. Dr. Welch got up and addressed the crowd.

"Well, I think Cheryl has said everything that needs to be said today."

Dr. Wilbur Welch was so in tune. He was astute. He let me say what I felt compelled to say, and for my emotions to come. Someone in his position could've brushed me off, or made me end my talk early, but Dr. Welch did not. Instead, he let me have the mic.

"I think she's spoken to our hearts, so I'm going to leave the altar open."

The response was profound.

How many times does that ever happen at a Christian college's chapel? I tell you—hardly ever! This is a community in which everyone has, supposedly, already given their lives to God. I looked down and tried to keep my eyes closed in honor of whatever God might choose to do in that moment. Fighting back tears, I felt exhausted by the moment. Telling the story was so draining. Being in front of that huge crowd had made me so nervous. And I realize now, God must have spoken through me because the response was profound.

Dr. Welch gave an "altar call." An altar call is when the pastor or speaker invites people to leave their seats and approach the altar or stage at the front of the church (or in this case, a makeshift podium in a gymnasium) for prayer. These times are usually reverent and emotional. Times when people pour out their soul's hurts before God, confess their sins, and receive the forgiveness He has promised us through Jesus.

Altar calls are also a public way for someone to make a commitment. Before their peers, friends, and community members, they are in effect saying, "I need to get right with God." You can imagine how reticent a room full of college kids would be to make such a public statement. However, the reaction to my story—really, to God's Spirit moving in people's hearts through my story—was *profound*. I looked down at the makeshift altar and saw that students—my peers, about one hundred or more—had come forward in chapel that day in order to make their lives right with God. It was amazing! Right there on a campus filled with Christians, God's Spirit moved to bring people to Him. I believe He convicted many to "stop playing the game" of being a Christian and to take His call on their lives seriously. Some even made confessions of faith in Jesus for the first time.

This event was emotional, nerve-racking, and energy-draining. However, it was a wonderful privilege for God to use me to spread the Gospel like this. This was one of the first of many times I would be blessed to see God change people's lives because of the story of the accident and the legacy of three people who were fully committed to serving God, even to the very end.

So as I say to so many people I talk with: *Stop, stop,* and be real with God! You never know what tomorrow holds or if you will still be breathing by tomorrow night. You do not have to be old to die. Trust me, I know.

Don't play the game, the Christian mask on for Sundays and your life as "hell" throughout the week. It is easy to do. I have done it too.

God knows all our hearts and He still loves us. Isn't that amazing! You are never, never too far from reach to reach out to God. He loves you and wants to be real with you! Please be real with Him. If you are mad, let Him know. If you are sad and depressed, talk to Him. I was for a time after the accident, and trust me, He is big enough to take it. So don't wait, do it today.

JIM AND DONNA COON ON CAMPUS

I wasn't the only one who was asked to address the student body at GRBC. Jim Coon was too. Here's another story from Jim. More of God's good work after the tragedy.

> The school asked me to address their student body in the gym. However, we arrived in Grand Rapids on Sunday. We attended the morning service [at a local church] and the pastor asked if I would tell our story in the evening service. I agreed.
>
> I had a letter in my coat pocket from a student thanking me for the "Sally Brochure."[15] It seems that this young man (a second-year student) was very concerned about his younger brother's relationship with the Lord and talked him into enrolling [at Grand Rapids Baptist College]. The younger brother picked up the brochure, and after reading it, started asking the older brother questions that soon led him to becoming a new believer! Therefore, his thank-you letter.
>
> While I spoke to the church that night, I reached into my pocket, pulled out the thank-you letter and read the story of these brothers to the congregation (while being careful not to divulge any names). At the conclusion of the service, a young man came to me and introduced himself as that younger brother! He also thanked me, which confirmed, once more, the purpose of this happening.

The next day, before the student body, my general theme was strengthening your faith for that day when the bottom falls out. (And it will, I promise!) The last thought I left with them was to guard your personal life. The things you do. The places you go. The things that (you think) are hidden. If God takes you home unexpectedly, someone will have to go through your personal effects. What will they find?

Amazing, as Jim says, "What is the purpose?" I think the Lord keeps showing us all these years. Many GMCs—God-Made Coincidences!

16

NOT BETTER,
BUT OKAY

I would like to share more from Mark's father, Dan Taube. Dan has a remarkable perspective about grief and about God.

"It just takes a while to come to grips with [death]. That . . . *it's okay*. It takes years to get to that feeling. It was a ten- or fifteen-year thing [after Mark's death]. It was bad . . . but it's okay."

Saying "it's okay" about the loss of a child is no small feat. How did he get to that place of peace? Dan shared with me the Taube family's story: "In 1981 New Tribes Mission moved us to Florida. When we were in Jackson [Michigan], everyone knew about Mark. But when we moved to a brand-new place, nobody knew the story." Dan said that you don't just tell new people about losing a child because it's so somber. It obviously takes time for a new relationship to deepen before you can share a story like that.

I think there were times when I just really didn't want to talk about it. In some cases, people just don't know about your son, so you don't tell them. What's to tell? Mark's friends in

Michigan were growing up and getting married and we just sort of lost all of that. We felt like part of the cost of losing a child is you don't get to see them grow up or do anything.

Each year on the Fourth of July Donna would make something special to eat. It was a somber day. While we knew Mark was on with the Lord, it takes a little while to be sure that it's really better for him to be on with the Lord than with us. [Dan chuckled at this.]

You expect to bury your parents, you don't expect to bury your children. But I've worked with plenty of people who have lost a child. Donna and I learned that we were far from the only people that have had to bury a child.

Who would he have married? What would he be like? We just missed out on all that stuff. It's the agony of loss. But here, more than forty years later, *being with the Lord becomes better and better* so the loss becomes, *not better, but it becomes okay.* It's okay. I don't recommend it for anybody but on the other hand, it's what the Lord had for me, *and it's okay.*

Donna Taube passed in 2015, which has added to Dan's perspective on grief and on God.

My wife has been with the Lord now better than seven years. I appreciate the fact that our Redeemer says, "I go to prepare a place for you that where I am ye may be also."[16] Donna is there and is set free from pain. She had a lot of pain during the last nineteen years of her life. Death is a blessing when you have a lot of pain. She was able to be carried on to be with the Lord. I'm doing fine as a widower, knowing who Jesus is. I can give clear testimony of that.

What an incredible testimony of faith in God! Dan continued:

> Every couple will have to bury someone. Either the wife will bury the husband, or the husband will bury the wife. Rarely do people die simultaneously. [He smiled and continued] Sometimes people feel like, "I've got a bad deal if my mate is dying." But really, [this perspective is] the flesh teaching us that we deserve to have good things. But it's just the reality of life. We don't have to *like* losing someone, but *it's okay* to have a loss. It's not *surprising.*"
>
> So, I consider myself blessed. Most of all because I was born in a place where the Gospel was preached. It's in my language and I've been able to read it all my life. And I like to talk about Jesus and what he did for me. It soon comes up in my conversation with people.
>
> Difficulties in life cause us to be drawn to the Lord in His goodness, or we can walk away and think "Poor me, I've had a bad time and I don't like it. Therefore, I'm going to be mad at God." If that wants to be our attitude, I predict a long unhappy life for anyone who walks that way.

These are *profound* words from someone who knows loss intimately. Yet Dan Taube continues to smile and laugh and just enjoy life.

> It all becomes better and better in my heart. My son is already with the Lord. My wife is with the Lord. I find a great deal of joy just in what the Lord has for me. Life has a lot of tribulation, *but that's okay*. Our Redeemer came and dealt with all matter of tribulation. I just consider myself very blessed.

Dan and I have corresponded and talked back and forth starting in the fall of 2021 after losing contact for a few years. Dan always ends his text, letters, or phone calls with "Our Redeemer Lives!" Yes sir, He does!

Mark Taube's death caused great grief for Dan, Donna, their family, and friends. It took time to sort through all the emotions of grief just like it does for many of us. With what all our world and all humanity has been through during the COVID-19 pandemic, world events, and losing so many friends and loved ones—how are you coping?

The Taube's were able to accept Mark's death because of their faith, a faith that believes "in all things God works for the good" (Romans 8:28). In addition to "Our Redeemer Lives!" Dan ends his texts, letters, and phone calls with these thoughts, "What a Redeemer/Shepherd Jesus is!" I hope you find the peace that you are looking for, as Mark's family did and still does.

THE FIRST TIME BACK AT LAKE ANN

In 2008, the Lord impressed upon me that it was finally time for me to go back to Lake Ann Camp. At the time, I hadn't been back since the accident—nearly thirty years. During the summer of 1982, I did not return to Lake Ann, but instead took a job working in Yellowstone National Park in Wyoming. My friend, mentor, and college basketball coach, Ray Gates, "Gator," first introduced me to the parks and took a group of us from college to work and live the summer in Yellowstone (Canyon Village).

My good friend and classmate Sandy Dow Haga roomed with me. Sandy is awesome and we all had such fun. (During the summer of 1982, I fell in love with the beauty of America's National Parks.) We took a college class, Ecology of Yellowstone, from my favorite professor. Throughout the summer, we hiked, explored, and examined the beauty of Yellowstone. After that summer ended, I began working for the National Park Service as a park ranger for the next ten seasons in parks such as Shiloh National Military Park, (I'm a history geek,) Cumberland Gap National Historical Park, and Great Smoky Mountains National Park, where I met my husband while working as a summer seasonal.

I later became a classroom teacher, mostly to middle school and high school students. I love teaching young people and have enjoyed teaching now thirty years. Along the way, I got married to my husband, Brad, and had two boys of my own.

So life was full and busy. I hadn't spent my life living in the summer of 1980. God had helped me move on. But in 2008 it was time to go back. I felt a prompting from God to do so. I wanted to go and see the camp and show it to my husband and our sons. I wanted them to see a place that had meant so much to me. I also wanted to remember, reflect, and make sure all the healing was done.

So, that spring I called the office. A man named E. J. Swanson, someone I didn't know, answered the phone. After a brief conversation, I'm told he yelled out to the rest of the staff that was present, "Does anyone know a Cheryl Steele Tinsley?"

I was surprised and thrilled to learn that my old friend, former college roommate, and co-counselor had recently taken an administrative position at the camp. (This was before social media and Facebook made it so easy to connect with old friends.) Gayle Yarick quickly got on the line and said, "Cheryl Steele Tinsley, get yourself up here." There's nothing like old friends!

So I planned my visit for that summer. Twenty-eight years is a long time. But I knew I needed to face things and bring the boys up to experience camp for themselves.

Gayle started reaching out to other friends, as well as Eldon Brock. When I finally returned to camp and gave my testimony, I was surrounded by people who knew my story and who had lived through the experience in their own ways. I was surrounded by people who truly cared.

It was also a great time for Eldon Brock and I to reconnect. "Dad Brock" was quiet. Sometimes a man of few words. He didn't always say things when he should have. After Dwight, Sally, and Mark passed, Dad Brock reached out to their families continually, but I didn't always feel like he was reaching out to me. It hurt. But honestly, I don't think he knew what to say. The whole situation was just *hard*. But this reunion in 2008 gave us a chance to talk things through. Our relationship started to heal after that, and it became a relationship I cherished until Eldon died in 2015. Just another way God moved and shared His grace after the tragedy.

What a blessing it has been to work and talk with young people and see them come to Christ at Lake Ann Camp again. Since that trip in 2008, I have returned each summer except two (heart surgery and COVID-19). And during each visit I have shared this story with campers and young counselors. Every time I do, I see God at work in people's lives. As I said, our lives are filled with God-Made Coincidences. I believe I was spared because my work on this earth was not yet finished. Why just me? Only God knows the answer to that question, and I trust him with it, and thank him for my life—*literally*.

I asked Gayle to share something she has learned during the years since the accident. She said, "God can use you in spite of *any* circumstance around you. He's got a plan and a purpose for your life." Gayle went on to describe what makes the Christian camp experience so special for kids:

I worked in the administration [for Lake Ann] from 2007–2010. I saw kids get burned out, or get frustrated, or not fit in at camp. Camp tends to be something kids think is wonderful or they want nothing to do with it. But despite the struggles, God works in *all* of those circumstances and situations. He has much for anybody to learn, [So, her hope and encouragement for campers has been] learn to be open. Have a heart that's open *for what God wants* you to learn. It may not be expected, but He has something for you.

17

ONE MORE MIRACLE

In the February of 2015, I was walking up the back staircase at Corbin High School and noticed that my heart was absolutely racing. I asked one of my coworkers to check my pulse and it was very high. I went to the doctor, and it was determined that I needed heart surgery. I was scheduled for an aortic valve replacement in order to correct something about my heart that I'd been born with.

My surgery was scheduled for May 12, 2015, at the Central Baptist Hospital in Lexington, Kentucky. At an appointment before the surgery, I met my surgeon and ended up telling him the story of the storm and the accident on Lake Huron. I also said to him, "You and I have a divine appointment, Doc."

This was a serious operation. It was open heart surgery that would stop my heart while sustaining my life with a machine. Though my surgeon had done over ten thousand of such surgeries, anything can happen in a surgery this serious. It was possible that I would not make it. As we've already seen, you never know what tomorrow will bring. So, before the surgery, I got all of my affairs in order. Also, all three of my sisters came to see me at the hospital. It was important that we see each other.

I told my sisters, "Look, if I don't make it off the table, girls, I've had a wonderful life. I've lived on God's time since I was twenty years old. So don't worry about me. I've gone on to be with the Lord." Among the group was my sister Carolyn, who, despite everything, was not a follower of Jesus. I said, "I'll see some of you on the other side," and gave them all hugs.

The whole night I was praying about the surgery. *Now listen, Lord, please don't take me out this way. After all I've been through, I still need to write that book.* I didn't really think that God was going to call me home. I just didn't feel that was going to happen. But it's a serious surgery, so I was praying. I was thinking about my husband, and my boys—how much I wanted to see them grow up, get married, have families of their own, and yes, grandchildren.

The next morning, I was feeling anxious and started praying, *God, you've just got to show me you're here. Show me you're here somehow.*

Nurses and assistants started to prep me for surgery. I quickly told them the story and said, "Please, when I get in there, if I start shaking, I'm not going into shock. I've had severe hypothermia." For someone who has had hypothermia as I have, shaking is not uncommon for the body during an experience like surgery.

So there I was, talking, talking, talking, as I'm being prepped for surgery. I was still feeling anxious and hoping God would show me he was there. That was when a beautiful Jamaican accent filled the room. My petite operating room nurse came through the door. Her name was Bethany. She had been listening in the adjacent room to my story about the accident, Lake Huron, and the freezing cold water. She put her hand on my hand and she said, "Cheryl, honey, I want you to know that you've got to just relax. You are a Type A personality. I can tell." She said it with a laugh. "Now slow down. Take a deep breath. Just relax and let us do our job." As soon as she touched me, I could just feel the presence of God. Yes, here was His sign.

Bethany said, "Baby, when you get up off of that gurney you're going to have another chapter for your book." I smiled and immediately felt my heart start to calm down.

Bethany left after that and they rolled me into the surgery room. While I was being given anesthesia, Bethany appeared again. "It's you!" I said, delighted.

She put her hand on mine and said, "You're going to wake up after this in ICU, and girl, you're going to write that next chapter."

I'd prayed for God to show me He was there, and He did!

When the surgery was all over, I started telling my sisters about Bethany. I told them all about how God had sent her, that she was there in the operating room, and how her touch and her words had just calmed me down. I knew and could feel that she was also a believer in Christ. Honestly, my sisters didn't know who I was talking about at all. They hadn't seen a petite nurse anywhere. They thought maybe the drugs I was given after surgery were talking.

Three days later, guess who walks in the door? It turns out the day after my surgery, Bethany had two days off. But when she returned to work, she came to visit me. I watched my sisters' jaws just *drop* when she came in the door.

"Cheryl, I wanted to come visit you," she said. "Cheryl, I believe in the Lord and the power of the Holy Spirit. And when you walked in, I felt it. And so, I just wanted to come back and tell you how much you blessed me that day."

While I was still in the hospital, Carolyn, who had witnessed everything—from our discussion before the surgery, to my description of Bethany, to Bethany's surprise appearance—said to me, "Sis, I want to know the peace that you had going into that surgery." There's only one answer for that: I have put my faith in Jesus as my Savior from sin and as the creator who loves me no matter what. Right there in the hospital I was able to lead my dear sister Carolyn to accept Christ into her life.

All those years ago, our mother had prayed while I was swimming for my life to Cockburn Island. She said, "let her live to live your legacy." Thirty-five years later, Carolyn and I were together, two sisters in prayer, living into the legacy of God— forgiveness, peace, joy. What a miracle!

I'd written a card to my surgeon and gave it to my husband, Brad. I asked Brad to give it to him whether the surgery was successful or not. I said, "If I don't make it, it's not his fault. God chose to take me home." And in the card I wrote to the doctor, "Whether I make it or not, I want to thank you for the skill that you have and that you have saved many people. I want you to know that God loves you dearly and has given you a gift, those surgeon hands of yours."

I was delighted to give it to him myself on the day they released me from the hospital. My wonderful, talented surgeon read the card and got teary-eyed. He gave me a hug and said, "Cheryl, you're one I won't forget. We *did* have a divine appointment."

A GIFT FROM DAD BROCK—DECADES LATER

As I've said already, Eldon "Dad" Brock was a mentor of mine. During his life he had a powerful, positive impact on undoubtedly thousands of campers, counselors, and staff members who made their way to Lake Ann, as well as his handpicked executive director (after he retired), Ken Riley.

Eldon and his wife, Trudy, were good at staying organized. Eldon meticulously saved personal letters, newspaper clippings, legal documents, and other items related to the accident. He gave them all to me just a few months before his death in August 2015. I'm going to share a few excerpts from this material because each excerpt demonstrates something about faith, the pain of loss, or what God was up to in the wake of the tragedy.

On July 8, 1980, just five days after Dwight's death, his mother, Bertie Herzberger, wrote a letter to Eldon Brock. This letter reveals the first of many ways Dwight, Sally, and Mark's deaths affected people far and wide.

> We are sending along the memorial offering given in Dwight's memory from the funeral and neighbors. We are expecting more but wanted to get this on its way so you can use it where you wish.
>
> We are trusting God and feeling peace from God, we do regret the awful tragedy and feel responsible. But, that would be taking God's place wouldn't it? As we know from His word, He is in control.
>
> I pray for the camp and all the staff, that it will have a great harvest and that Dwight's (and the others') testimony will be a source of encouragement.
>
> God bless you all in Jesus — Bertie (and Bud) Herzberger

Eldon added a note to this letter in the bottom corner: "$960 enclosed." This may or may not seem like a lot of money in today's world, but I suspect it was a generous donation for a small Christian camp to have received in 1980. It's a small testament to how God can use a terrible tragedy to motivate people to dedicate what they have to good work.

This letter also reveals a strong faith on the part of the Herzbergers. Just five days after she lost her son, a grieving mother can say, "God is in control" in the middle of emotions that obviously conflicted within her. What a testament of faith!

In another letter to Eldon Brock—this one dated September 24, 1980, a little less than three months after the accident—Mark's father, Dan Taube, said the following:

> Events in life occur with stunning swiftness, what a blessing to know the Lord . . .
>
> Cheryl was here for a couple of hours last Saturday night. We had a good visit. She told us of the article in the *National Enquirer* . . .
>
> We recently received the yearbook from Jackson Baptist [high school] for the '79–'80 school year. It has a number of good pictures of both Mark and Dwight. Pictures bring great joy and at the same time the pain of grief becomes a little sharper.

Bertie Herzberger also wrote a letter to Eldon and Trudy on September 24, 1980. Their letter includes the following:

> This letter is long overdue and comes with my apologies (again). I find it so difficult to finalize Dwight's life and things concerning [the] tragedy.

You mentioned a "portrait type" picture of Dwight. Don't I wish we had just that, but he wasn't usually serious for a picture—you know how his humor was.

God is working in lives here. We are being comforted daily and people are still praying for us faithfully. We are able to trust in our Lord daily and He is keeping us super busy.

We had a nice visit with Cheryl Steele on her way home from camp in August. She stayed one night and we talked 'til 3:30 a.m. If I hadn't had to go to work the next day we would have gone on all night.

Eldon had evidently performed some of the necessary duties of identification after the bodies were found because Bertie also said:

I'm enclosing a check . . . hoping this will help cover some of the expense of plane fare, etc. to identify our children for us. I can't tell you what a great relief it was when you did that for us. You actually took the pain upon yourself for us, one we can never repay, just say "thank you," "bless you" and may our lovely Lord heal the wound.

Hoping to see you soon—you are in our prayers also— thank you for remembering us in prayer—we need it!

God bless you both, love in Christ, Bertie and Bud Herzberger

So much is contained in this short note from Bertie. God was continuing to work in the lives of people in their community. This was a couple of months after the outpouring of donations for the camp at Dwight's funeral. His loss was greatly felt by his students and other teachers, and God was perhaps using this loss as an introduction for people to hear about Jesus—the one in whom Dwight had placed his trust.

This note also speaks to Eldon's character. He did the unhappy work of legally identifying the bodies of Dwight, Sally, and Mark. (At that time, I was likely in one of the two hospitals I visited and in no shape for speaking with authorities.)

Lastly, this letter reveals the continued, often conflicting, feelings all believers feel when faced with loss of a loved one—especially a sudden loss. While we place our confidence and trust in God, the pain of grief is severe. This is not easy to experience. In many ways it is the proving ground of faith.

Later that fall, Mark's mother, Donna, sent another note to Eldon Brock after he'd gone to visit the Taubes.

> Needless to say, it is not easy, and the Lord gives grace daily to us . . . [we] continue to miss Mark very much at times.
>
> The other day we had a card from Family Life Radio saying someone had sent in a memorial gift in Mark's name.

Family Life Radio is a ministry that continues today and has affected the lives of millions of listeners over the years. It's amazing to think that Mark's death was used by God to help continue this important ministry at that time. We may not always see the ripple effects of the things we endure, but God has proven that he can bring good out of even the most awful circumstances.

HE BEING DEAD YET SPEAKETH

Among the materials Eldon gave me was a camp newsletter that was sent sometime in the latter half of 1980. It was sent to churches that supported the Regular Baptist Camp at Lake Ann, as well as other donors and friends of the camp. The letter was entitled "Tragedy Or Victory At Lake Ann Camp" and it recounts the story. It includes the following quotes:

> Depending on the observer's point of view, A survey trip to Drummond Island by four staff members of the Baptist Camp, Lake Ann, Michigan, ended in victory or tragedy.
>
> Cheryl Steele, age 20, survived 15 hours in the cold waters of Lake Huron while three companions died in an attempt to overcome strong winds and a long night of darkness. The tragedy, in our human eyes, has been a victory for the three who entered heaven during the night of July 3, 1980. Also, it is becoming a victory for God as the example of all four takes effect because of their lives and the shocking experience of survival and death.

This letter's title gives away the perspective that Eldon Brock and the others at Lake Ann had about this accident—a perspective I have been thankful for over the years. It was a terrible accident. The loss of Dwight, Sally, and Mark is severe. Yet upon their deaths, they experienced *victory*. They were ushered into the kingdom of God because of Jesus's victory over sin. Their faith in Him brought them into God's presence, where no storm can ever threaten them again.

The newsletter continued:

> Reports are still coming in on how God has used this tragedy to fulfill His promise of Romans 8:28. As to be expected, the Camp has evaluated the programs even more than usual. Many have reviewed their lives to see what kind of testimony they would leave if suddenly taken. There are reports of many opening to witness and some have accepted Christ as Saviour.

No one would ask God for an experience like this, but none of those involved would want to give up the lessons learned from God who has shown Himself in many special ways as He promised in the Scriptures. Like Abel (Hebrews 11:4b "He being dead yet speaketh"),[17] the righteous works and the talents of each will influence many to trust in God.

Hebrews 11 is a chapter that has been often called "The Hall of Faith." It's a chapter near the end of the Bible, in the New Testament, which lists a number of people from across history that showed extraordinary faith in God. Many of these people experienced incredible suffering in their lives too. Some died tragically.

This particular quote in the newsletter—"He being dead yet speaketh"—is not just a funny way of talking about death. It's about the legacy one leaves behind. It's referring to a story about the too-early death of another young person, Abel. Abel was one of the first two sons of Adam and Eve. Abel was killed by his brother, Cain, who flew into a jealous rage when God accepted Abel's offering and not his own. Even after Abel's death, his legacy seemed to "cry out" to God.[18]

After the "Hall of Faith" comes to a close, Hebrews 12 begins with these verses:

> Therefore, since we are surrounded by such a huge crowd of witnesses to the life of faith, let us strip off every weight that slows us down, especially the sin that so easily trips us up. And let us run with endurance the race God has set before us. We do this by keeping our eyes on Jesus, the champion who initiates and perfects our faith.[19]

This is the perspective I have to this day. Like the staff at Lake Ann, I remember that even though Dwight, Sally, and Mark were taken from us too soon, their sin was conquered by the death and resurrection of Jesus. When they died, sin and evil did not win. Instead, God brought them home to be with him. That is their legacy—God's victory over sin. In their memories, and in recognition of God's victory, we who are here on earth should "run with endurance the race God has set before us," and keep our eyes on Jesus.

He being dead yet speaketh, indeed!

CONCLUSION

TIMELESS TRUTHS

I don't call this "my story" because I think it's God's story. It's a story about His love, His faithfulness, and His immense power to change lives, even in tragic circumstances.

This story is as much mine as it is Dwight Herzberger, Sally Coon, and Mark Taube's. I've often said that when I get to heaven, I'm going to see Mom and Dad first, with Dwight, Sally, and Mark right behind them. I am going to give them all a long hug . . . and my first question to my friends will be, "Did you see from your perspective the impact your lives and death had on earth?"

They're in the presence of Jesus right now. Anyone who trusts in Him for salvation will have the opportunity to meet them there too. (If you openly declare that Jesus is Lord and believe in your heart that God raised Him from the dead, you will be saved. "For it is by believing in your heart that you are made right with God, and it is by openly declaring your faith that you are saved" (Romans 10: 9-11, NLT)).

To close this book, I want to share some timeless truths I have learned during the course of my life.

1. You are not on this earth by accident. I don't care what anybody's told you. You are not an accident. You were created by the Lord God Almighty—you were fearfully and wonderfully made!

   "Thank you for making me so wonderfully complex! Your workmanship is marvelous—how well I know it" (Psalms 139:14 NLT).

2. God loves you more than you'll ever know. He even knows the number of hairs on your head. How cool is that! He is a God of all-knowing and details.

   "And the very hairs on your head are all numbered. So don't be afraid; you are more valuable to God than a whole flock of sparrows" (Luke 12:7 NLT).

3. Don't wait until tomorrow to get right with God. Tomorrow may never come for you.

   "How do you know what your life will be like tomorrow? Your life is like the morning fog—it's here a little while, then it's gone" (James 4:14 NLT).

4. Don't ever, ever stand over a grave with regrets in your heart. Let go of the hurt that is in your heart, forgive, and let God handle it. You can be honest with God. He loves you and you can be real with Him—yell, scream, get it out, talk to Him. My friend, you have a choice either to be bitter, or to be better.

   "Don't worry about anything; instead, pray about everything. Tell God what you need, and thank him for all he has done. Then you will experience God's peace, which exceeds anything we can understand. His peace will guard your hearts and minds as you live in Christ Jesus" (Philippians 4:6–7 NLT).

He is always beside if you let Him be present with you throughout this earthly life. As well as when you open your eyes after your last breath on earth. I do so believe you will look into the eyes of Jesus just like my friends did when they took their last breath on this earth.

I love this quote from the author C. S. Lewis: "Friendship is born at that moment when one person says to another: 'What! You too? I thought I was the only one.'"

My friend,
I told it to you straight, all details, emotions, and events as I lived them, just like I promised on the first page of this book, *Wave by Wave*.
I hope I made you think . . .
God's Blessings,
Cheryl Steele Tinsley

ACKNOWLEDGMENTS

To the "hunky" guy I met at Sugarlands Visitor's Center while we worked in the Great Smoky Mountains National Park, my best friend and husband, Brad. I am forever grateful to the Lord for you—your love, humor (you still make me laugh), your kindness, love for the Lord, and your strength. You have always been my rock!

To my two sons, Robbie Tinsley and Jeff Tinsley. Being your Mom is the BEST and the best title I could have ever obtained on this earth. What fun and great joy it has been to be able to watch you grow up and become the awesome young men you are! Always follow God's leading and remember:

I'll love you forever
I'll like you for always
As long as I'm living
My babies you'll be.

To my lifelong besties, we all have shared so many adventures and life challenges together:

Robin Brandenburg Elliott
Julie Webster Gardinour
Sandy Dow Haga
Kim Brunan Manzer
Melissa "Shack"
Kim Shoebridge (1959-2016)
Lynn Carl Stivers
Gayle Yarick

You all are my "tribe." I love you ladies and can never thank each of you enough for all your love, support (for me and family), all the crazy, fun times and encouragement all these years. I want you to know what a gift each of your friendships are to me!

To Dr. Ray "Gator" Gates (Cornerstone University), my wonderful professor, mentor, and friend. I want to thank you for introducing me to God's beautiful creation through working out West and doing the Ecology of Yellowstone the summer of 1982. Gator, because you introduced me to the beauty of our national parks, I met my husband Brad a few years later in the Smokies! You always checked on me, prayed for and encouraged me, especially during those healing years in college after the accident, and even today. I want you to know the profound impact you have had in my life! I thank the Lord for your friendship and that you had enough sense to marry your lovely wife, Carol, after all us girls checked her out and gave her the "thumbs up" in Yellowstone the summer of 1982.

To Jim and Donna Coon and their families, Bertie and Bud Herzberger and their families, Dan and Donna Taube and their families. My sincere love and tremendous thanks to all for your help with this book, your prayers, and love toward me these many years. Not a month has gone by in my life since the summer of 1980 that I have not prayed for you and your families. Each of you had to endure the loss of a child and then turn your grief toward heaven for healing. Your strength and steadfast faith have been seen by so many people all these years. I know you all will stand one day in heaven and have lines of people behind you. They will be there because of your testimony and faith in God. You all are the "walking examples" of Roman 8:28 throughout your lives.

Thank you to Jim Coon! He was the first one I contacted about this book, and he agreed to add to it from his family's perspective. The more he wrote, the more God gave him insights that he calls, "What is the Purpose?" He is currently writing a book about God's faithfulness and purpose in all things in life. Also, Jim and his daughter Carol Coon Ulrich came to Lake Ann Camp this past July 2022 to see me. Jim spoke to the Reborne Rangers and walked up a steep hill in Sleeping Bear Dunes National Lakeshore. Jim beat me up the hill as a ninety-year-old! He is such a remarkable man and so funny. He always makes me laugh.

Thank you to Dan Taube, as he also agreed to talk to Andy Rogers and included his and his family's perspective throughout the years. (Finally, after meeting his nephew Rick, I was able to obtain Dan's current cell number and caught up with Dan with a phone call back in August. He had to call me back as he was showing livestock at the Iowa State Fair that day. That cracked me up. It just shows no matter what your age you've got to keep active and do the things you enjoy.)

Eldon Brock and his family (Eldon makes his home in heaven now). Thank you, Eldon! Had it not been for Eldon and Trudy's tremendous insight to save every newspaper article, official reports, cards, and everything else about the accident, there is no way I could have written *Wave by Wave*.

To Ken Riley, the executive director of Lake Ann Camp, Lake Ann, Michigan. Ken, you have been a friend to me and an outstanding leader for decades. Eldon Brock could not have picked anyone better than you and your beautiful family to lead the ministry. Lake Ann Camp has grown and reached thousands for Christ during these last (almost forty) years under your leadership.

Also, Ken for all your insight and contribution to the book about our friend and your mentor Dwight Herzberger—thank you!

My buddy Jeff Tindall, who has been my friend all these years. Only you, Jeff, know our adventures and laughter with Dwight. During all the tears those first few years after the accident, you always listened and prayed as I talked about Dwight, Sally, Mark, and the accident through the stages of grief and then healing. You are amazing, my wonderful friend!

To my mom, Edna Steele, and my dad, Earl Steele. For all your guidance, prayers, love, and patience toward your youngest daughter. God blessed me with the best parents! You always encouraged me to be myself and "go for it" and never look back at life with regrets. "Always Reach for the Stars, and give 100%," my dad used to say. And Mom, you were the absolute best! Family and friends knew your love and that everything you touched was better off because of it. You were both "Always the Wind Beneath my Wings."

To my wonderful siblings: JoAnn Hammons, Carolyn Steele, Linda Steele, Jim Steele, and Earl Alan Steele (1964–2019). Thank you for all your love and support through our growing up years and adulthood. Thank you for all your encouragement. Love you all.

And lastly, my beautiful friends Dwight Herzberger, Sally Coon, and Mark Taube. The book is dedicated to you three amigos of mine. One day, I will stand on the shores of heaven with you! We will walk together again, talking, laughing, and singing praises to God!

This book has been on the back burners of my mind for many years. I was praying and waiting for God's timing for a few years. I am so thankful that my friend Ray Gates introduced me to his colleague from Cornerstone University, Mr. Mark Tremaine. Mark came up to Lake Ann Camp and met my husband, Brad, and me in the summer 2021 while I was speaking at camp. What was to be an hour meeting turned into five hours and a wonderful dinner. Mark taped my testimony, kept stopping his tape and said "WOW!" "Unbelievable!" "Amazing!" "Cheryl, you must get your story into print." Mark in turn introduced me to a friend of his who also graduated from Cornerstone University (our awesome alma mater), Tim Beals of Credo House Publishers, who later introduced me to my ghostwriter, Andy Rogers (also a Cornerstone alum). After talking to both Tim and Andy separately (later followed by a joint conversation), I said: "I have been waiting to meet the right people that God would send to write my story and publish the book for years, and I just did."

My sincere thanks to Andy Rogers for countless hours on the phone, asking questions and writing this book, and to Tim Beals for his publishing expertise to put it into print. I could not have done any of this without you both.

I am grateful for my life that was spared in the frigid waters of Lake Huron many years ago. I am a "Miracle Baby," as that handsome doctor said so many years ago. But it was God who performed the miracle. There is no other reason I lived to tell about it.

> Jesus looked at them intently and said, "Humanly speaking, it is impossible. But with God everything is possible.
> (Matthew 19:26 NLT)

—Cheryl Steele Tinsley

This book was written during the summer of 2022, forty-two years after the tragedy on July 3, 1980. It has been an enormous privilege to write this story with Cheryl Steele Tinsley within, as she would say, "God's timing" for the book. Her enthusiasm and sense of humor made the process of collaboration a joy. Thank you, Cheryl, for the countless hours you spent on the phone answering my questions. Thank you, also, for the wealth of documents, photos, and other information you provided along the way.

I also owe a large debt of gratitude to the numerous others who allowed me to interview them for this book and who sent me written material as well: Jim Coon, Dr. Ray Gates, Sandy Dow Haga, Ken Riley, Dan Taube, Carole Coon Ulrich, and Gayle Yarick. Each of you filled in gaps in the story and added vivid detail about the three amazing people who were lost. Thank you.

Lastly, I want to thank Tim Beals for introducing me to Cheryl, and my wife and children for their support and love.

—A. L. Rogers

ENDNOTES

1. Unbeknownst to Eldon and Dan Taube, Mark falsified some of the information he gave the camp, saying he was eighteen years old instead of seventeen in order to qualify for the death benefit the camp's insurance would provide should something tragic happen. Most of us thought he was eighteen that summer.

2. Image of the North Channel from Wikimedia Commons, by P199 — Derivative from image:Great_Lakes_Lake_Huron_Georgian_Bay.png, Public Domain, commons.wikimedia.org/w/index.php?curid=5129420.

3. For a comparison of the largest lakes in the world, visit www.visual capitalist.com/worlds-25-largest-lakes/. Lake Huron is fourth on the list.

4. We would later learn that Dwight's wristwatch stopped at fifteen minutes before 2 p.m.

5. www.cdc.gov/disasters/winter/staysafe/hypothermia.html. Accessed February 14, 2022.

6. www.mayoclinic.org/diseases-conditions/hypothermia/symptoms-causes/syc-20352682. Accessed August 2022.

7. There are two women named Donna in this story. Mark's mother, Donna Taube, and Sally's mother, Donna Coon.

8. Ken Bradstreet's story has been copied from the funeral brochure. Reprinted with permission.

9. Chris Jenkins, "Christian daughter's testimony lives on," *Herald Times*, July 10, 1980, 3.

10. Exodus 20:16, "You must not testify falsely against your neighbor," New Living Translation.
11. John 14:6, New International Version.
12. Hebrews 6:18, New Living Translation.
13. John 8:44, New Living Translation.
14. When the Mol Arena opened in 2000, this facility became the "blue gym," a secondary practice space for the Cornerstone University athletics program.
15. The pamphlet containing Kenneth Bradstreet's story.
16. John 14:3; read verses 1–4 for the full context.
17. Hebrews 11:4, King James Version.
18. You can read the full story of Cain and Abel in the first book of the Bible. Genesis 4:1–16.
19. Hebrews 12:1–2, New Living Translation.

Made in the USA
Las Vegas, NV
15 March 2023

69116750R00098